MW00932567

Refuse

To

Drown

Tim Kreider

with Shawn Smucker

© 2013 Refuse To Drown LLC

All rights reserved. No part of this book may be reproduced or transmitted in any from or by any means, electronic or mechanical, including photocopying, recording, or by any information storage or retrieval system, without permission in writing from the copyright holders.

For more information on Also-Me, please see www.also-me.org

Edited by Andi Cumbo
Cover design by Jason McCarty

To Lynn,

Your unwavering love, support, and strength
continue to amaze and
inspire me to be a better man.
I thank God every day
for the blessing of you in my life.

Tim

Many of the names in this book have been changed to protect the identities of the people involved in the story.

Table of Contents

Introduction

Why write this book?

I know it's a question a lot of people will ask. Some may think it's inappropriate for the father of a convicted killer to revisit a story that still holds so much pain for so many people. Others will question my motives, perhaps thinking I'm hoping to profit from the tragedy, either through fame or fortune.

I can understand such sentiments.

Initially, writing about these events was simply a therapeutic process. It was a way to release some of the anguish I felt, a way to express my emotions on paper in a way I couldn't verbally. There was something raw about putting everything into the written word, but there was also healing in that process. Once it seemed to have run its course, I put what I had written aside and began the hard work of putting my life back together. But a quiet voice spoke to me during the last few years, and I don't feel like I can ignore it any longer.

What if, by sharing your story, you can prevent this from happening to other families? What if, by sharing your story, it will help someone find a way to get through a difficult time? Is there a message of hope and redemption that can be a lifesaver for someone?

My son believed that he had to handle his internal struggles on his own. There were many reasons he felt this way. In part, I contributed to this feeling by telling him that he must take responsibility for his actions and his anger. In an effort to get him to realize the importance of accountability, I inadvertently sent a message to him that he was expected to handle what he was going through on his own. It was not my intention, but I think that was the message he received.

Of course, there were other underlying issues: he didn't think anyone would understand what he was going through; he thought that if he did share his pain, people might ridicule him or think he was a freak. But it was this internal struggle and continued secrecy that eventually led him to commit a terrible act. In the silence and secrecy of his own heart, anger and hatred grew unchecked.

And I'm left wondering.

What if he had gone for help earlier?

What if he had shared his struggles with a counselor?

What if he had realized that he wasn't alone?

This is why I wrote this book.

To those who feel isolated and hopeless – you're not alone.

To those who are depressed or angry or suicidal – you're not alone.

To those whose children struggle with anger, depression, or a mental illness – you're not alone.

For each one of us, there's a right way, and there's an easy way, and they're rarely the same path. Think about the choices you are making. Think about the path you are on. Believe it or not, trying to go alone or make your own way or handle your problems internally is the easy way. It's hard to step forward and ask for help. It's difficult to admit that you're struggling when everyone around you seems to have it so together. Don't let this perception fool you. Everyone has struggles, doubts, and fears at some time in their life.

I don't say that to diminish what you are going through, but simply to let you know that you don't need to be ashamed of your situation. You're not alone, no matter what the circumstances. Somewhere, at some time, someone went through what you are experiencing. They faced it and conquered it, and so can you.

Please. Don't wait any longer. Whether you are a parent of a struggling child, a young person who feels like life is a battle, or anyone else who feels lost and alone: reach out for help.

Do it now!

Maybe you're on the other side of the equation. Maybe you're emotionally strong and mentally aware. Then, help others. This is your call to action – reach out to someone today and let them know they're not alone. When we were in the middle of this tragedy, we received countless letters and notes, encouraging words that helped me get through one more minute, one more hour, one more day. These were the threads of hope in what seemed to be a hopeless situation, a flicker of light in the darkness of my life. Never underestimate the power of a caring action or compassionate word. They have the power to change a life. They have the power to change the world.

Why write this book?

Could my story help someone avoid tragedy? Could reading my story be the impetus for someone to finally get help? Could these words be the tipping point for parents to confront their teenager? Could my personal journey from utter darkness to the light at the other side help, inspire, or guide someone else?

I hope so. That's why I wrote this book: in the hope that tragedies such as this one can be prevented.

You're not alone.

1

Too Close to Home

On a chilly Friday night in mid-May, I walked upstairs and got ready for bed. The house felt quiet. My three children were over at their mother's house and my fiancé Lynn had just gone home. My dog, a boxer named Knock Out, stretched and then crept behind me up the stairs like a shadow. In the midst of that quiet, my mind moved restlessly from here to there: work was hectic as usual, Lynn and I were planning our August wedding, and my teenage kids, with their sports and activities and jobs, had me hustling just to keep up.

But something happened later that night, after I fell asleep, something that would change my life and shatter the serenity of our small community.

It started when someone eased their way through the back door of a house at the top of a small hill. Large, mature trees lined that tranquil street, and the house's backyard ran right up against the backyards of other houses, which faced other streets. Even from the outside of the gray and white house, you could tell the family who lived there led well-kept, organized, peaceful lives.

The intruder must have known where to go, because, in spite of the close proximity of the surrounding homes, no one reported anything out of the ordinary. There was no forced entry. There didn't have to be, since the family in the gray stone house left their doors unlocked – just an example of the kind of neighborhood they lived in. Lynn, my fiancé, had just gotten on my case for leaving the doors to my own house unlocked, but to be honest I didn't take her warnings very seriously. Nothing that bad ever happened.

But on that night, someone snuck inside that house and stabbed 16-year-old Kevin Haines and his parents, 50-year-old Thomas, a salesman at a local industrial supply store, and 47-year-old Lisa, a pre-school teacher. The Haines' 20-year-old daughter, home a few days earlier than expected from college, slept in her room and was left untouched. She woke up in the middle of the night and smelled blood. She found her parents. Her mother told her to run for help, so she did, but it was too late.

Hours earlier, as I prepared for sleep, I had no sense of foreboding. I brushed my teeth and crawled into bed. I read for a few minutes; then, I turned off the light. It was the last night I ever went to bed in that house without locking the doors.

The place where I lived, Manheim Township, Pennsylvania, has a population of around 30,000 and is a suburban area between the town of Lititz and Lancaster City. Manheim Township is one of the more upscale, suburban neighborhoods in the county, always maintaining one of the finest school districts. It's a quiet, middle- to upper-middle class place where the biggest concerns most kids have are whether or not they'll make the varsity soccer team or who they'll go with to the prom.

Of course, it's not completely ideal, and our kids face the same issues all kids face: peer pressure and partying and dealing with parents' expectations. But the crime rate stays low, and if the police get a call, it seems like it's usually a minor car accident or some of the locals causing mischief.

Sometimes, it's so quiet it can seem downright boring – most of the neighborhoods have few, if any, through streets, so the traffic stays on the main roads. It's unusual for a car that I don't recognize to drive past my house, and there's this friendly peer-pressure: if one neighbor mows their grass, everyone else feels like they have to as well. There have been a few isolated incidents, tragic stories that take your breath away with their horror and leave you shaking your head, looking for answers. But nothing close to home.

Until that chilly night in May.

The person who killed Kevin and his parents walked out the rear sliding-glass door of their house, leaving it partially open and vanishing into the darkness. Only a few bloody footprints remained. No one knew this at the time, but the killer fled to a home less than half a mile from the Haines' residence.

This is the story of what followed, the story of the weeks that came after the Haines family was murdered, during which the crime went unsolved. Most of us had trouble falling asleep. I was concerned for my daughter, my two sons, Lynn, and my ex-wife. The person or people who had done this were still out there. Where were they? Would they strike again? I lay in bed, and my heart raced at every small sound.

Was that someone messing with the locks...or was it just my imagination?

Did I just hear a door open?

Was that one of my kids going to the bathroom in the middle of the night...or is someone sneaking up the stairway?

No motive? Nothing stolen? We all wondered who could have done it. We all hoped they would be found quickly.

But I had no idea how the discovery of the identity of this particular criminal would change my life.

2

Typical Alec

It seemed a normal Saturday in May: I didn't have to go to work, everything started on a nice, relaxing note, and I had a few non-pressing things on my to-do list that needed attention. Yet, now I remember many things about that particular day, things you normally wouldn't remember about a Saturday years in the past. For instance, I remember the date: it was the 12th of May.

I arrived at my ex-wife's house a little after noon to pick up my daughter, Amy. They lived in a townhouse, an end unit, not far from where Lynn and I were taking her out for a belated birthday lunch. Amy worked a lot of hours, and I looked forward to spending quality time with her, but I don't recall our intended lunch destination. Those details no longer hold any importance.

It was one of those beautiful late spring days: a blue sky, slight breeze, and a coolness hiding the fact that summer was just around the corner.

I knocked on the door. My daughter answered. She's about 5' 3" with longer, dark-brown hair, a beautiful smile, and a vibrant personality. She had been out of high school for a year and was still in that searching phase that so many of us go through in our late teen years. I could immediately tell that she had been crying.

"Hey, what's wrong?" I asked.

At first, she shook her head. Then, she spoke.

"Someone killed Kevin," she squeezed a tissue in her hands and sniffed her nose.

"Kevin who?" I asked, assuming it was someone I didn't know.

"You know," she said. "Kevin. Alec's friend."

Alec is my oldest son. He was 16-years-old at the time.

"Kevin!" I replied, shocked, not believing. "Are you sure?"

An image of Kevin flashed through my mind. I had first met him when he was in the 4th or 5th grade, maybe even younger. He was a quiet kid, extremely bright and involved in his church and the Boy Scouts.

"Look at these kids," I had told Lynn a few months before. "They're almost taller than I am! It seems like yesterday they were just little boys, and now they're so grown up!" Even at that point though, Kevin had a baby face. He was polite and kind – I had never seen him any other way.

It turns out there was a front-page story about the murders in the Saturday morning newspaper. Kevin Haines and his parents had been killed in their home during the night. Only his sister had escaped. Like everyone else who heard the story, I couldn't believe it. I had seen Kevin and his father on Thursday evening at a meeting regarding a trip to Germany organized by the school. Thursday evening! Not even two days ago. Kevin and Alec were going to be roommates on the trip. The weekend before that, Kevin had been at our house. Plus, the Haines family lived just up the street from where I was standing, probably half a mile away.

I didn't know what to say to my daughter, so I just hugged her.

"Are you okay?" I asked her.

"Kevin and his parents were such nice people. He was such a good kid. It doesn't make any sense," she said. "Who would want to hurt them?"

I didn't have any answers for her. I wondered the same thing.

"How's Alec doing?" I asked.

He and Kevin were close friends. The two of them, along with one other young man, spent a lot of time together. I had watched all three of them change and grow up during the previous five or six years. By that spring, they were sophomores in high school, growing into young men and planning their futures.

I referred to them as "The Three Musketeers". The fact that one of them was gone was unimaginable.

"Mom already talked to Alec," my daughter said. "He's up in his room."

Then, I thought of my youngest son, Drew. He knew Kevin and played video games with the boys when they were at our place. My daughter told me that he was at a friend's house and probably hadn't heard the news, and I was relieved he didn't have to witness all of us finding out – it would give me some time to process what had happened. I turned my focus back to Alec.

"Are you sure Alec is okay?" I asked Amy.

"He'll be fine," she assured me.

"I should check on him," I said.

She nodded.

Thoughts raced through my head as I walked up the stairs to Alec's room. I was still in the act of processing what I had just heard. I thought more about the Haines family. They were quiet and unimposing. Kevin's dad was tall, about my height, with a runner's build. Walking into their home had always been like walking onto the set of *Leave it to Beaver*. I don't mean that in a negative way at all. Everything was clean, neat, and organized. They were all polite, sincere, and loving. They were always on time, and by all appearances, formed a strong family unit.

Who would ever want to hurt them?

As I approached the top of the steps, I started to have serious concerns for Alec. The past twelve months had already been tough on him. He seemed to be in a constant fight with his mood and emotions, and he put heavy pressure on himself over school and his grades. He was tired all the time and even seemed depressed. But no matter how I approached him, he wouldn't open up, and he refused to speak to a counselor.

In my mind, this tragedy was another stress he would have to face, and I didn't know how he would handle it.

I got to the top of the steps. The door to his room was closed. I knocked lightly.

A barely audible "Yeah?" came from inside.

"Hey, dude, are you okay? May I come in?"

"Yeah."

I opened the door and found Alec curled up on his bed, crying. His backpack was on the floor beside him. I walked slowly across the room to his bed. He had short brown hair and brown eyes, and a trace of stubble was beginning to show on his chin. He was somewhere between childhood and manhood, and it had been a rough journey up to that point.

I sat with him and put my arm around him, trying to give him some kind of comfort. He didn't totally accept my sympathy – he remained withdrawn, but this was typical Alec.

I'll be fine, I don't want to talk about it was generally the vibe he gave off, but that had always been his way of doing things. He wasn't a touchy-feely kid.

He seemed exhausted and unable to discuss what he had heard. This didn't seem strange to me: after all, the news was shocking, and Kevin was his close friend. We didn't say much. I knew nothing that I said would heal things. So I just stayed beside him and put my hand on his shoulder

"Why don't you come back home with me for the afternoon?" I asked. His mother wouldn't be home for a few hours, and I didn't think he should be home alone. As far as I knew, the killer or killers hadn't been found yet, and even apart from that, I could tell my kids needed some emotional support.

"Yeah, that sounds good," he said, sounding relieved. While he put on his shoes, I went downstairs and asked my daughter if she wanted to come with us. She also welcomed the invitation, and we decided to postpone her birthday lunch, at least temporarily. I was glad they agreed – I wanted to help both of them in any way I could and make them feel safe. I also wanted to keep an eye on Alec. I was concerned about his emotional state.

My house was only a few minutes away, but it seemed much longer in the uncomfortable quiet of the ride. Everyone attempted to digest the tragic news. Who could have done it? Why the Haines family? Questions spun around and around inside my head.

I thought back to a few weekends before, when Kevin had come over. I had taken Kevin and my two boys to my grandparents' house and then to my cousin's – both lived in the country, and the boys had a lot of time and space to run around and explore. It had been one of those wonderful days when you know that the sunshine and freedom of summer are just around the corner.

I was on friendly terms with Kevin's father – we both ran, a common theme of discussion for us. Every once in a while, I'd see him running through our neighborhood.

Now, Kevin and his parents were dead. Even worse, murdered.

I called Lynn on my way to the house.

"We're not going to lunch," I told her. "Something bad has happened."

"What?" she asked me, concerned.

"Someone killed Kevin Haines and his parents."

Disbelief filled her voice.

"I'll meet you at home," she said.

When we arrived at the house, a somber air followed us inside. Lynn stepped outside so that I could spend some time alone with the kids. This was a very personal issue for my family, and she realized that we might need some time to talk. Alec looked confused and drained. He lay down on the couch, and I checked on my daughter again.

"How could this happen?" she kept asking. "Why would anyone do this?"

How can you answer questions such as these?

"I don't know," I said. "It doesn't make any sense to me either."

After about 20 minutes, Lynn came back inside.

"Do you want to go outside and talk a little bit?" she asked Amy, who nodded, so the two of them went outside and sat in the yard with their backs against a tree. My daughter vacillated between crying and saying, "I don't understand!"

Meanwhile, inside the house, I moved over to the couch and sat down with Alec. He put his feet on my lap, seeming to need my presence and quiet reassurance. We sat there like that for quite some time, quietly, as if waiting for something.

I watched him closely, thinking back over some of the things we had been through with Alec. He had been dealt a tough hand in life: he had issues with his eyes from birth, needed surgery before he was a year old, and we spent much of his boyhood trying to get him to wear his glasses. When he was a toddler, he was bitten on the face by a dog and required numerous stitches. After that, whenever he got angry, the scar turned bright red.

When he was a little older, he needed braces and was self-conscious about how they looked. He was so proud of his smile when the braces were removed. It was less than a year after this that he significantly chipped both of his front teeth while playing in a pool. The perfect teeth were no more.

Once he hit school, he never had many close friends. He struggled to understand the world, and his constant analysis of people's behavior always fell short of providing him with an explanation of why people did what they did. It seemed that throughout his life he struggled with anger, even more so in recent years.

I often thought a significant source of his anger came from an inability to emotionally understand why things weren't the way he thought they should be. Why didn't people just act the way they're supposed to and do the things they should? He became frustrated and then angry at these types of situations and the people involved.

Prior to that day, Lynn and I had become increasingly concerned, on multiple levels, with how he was doing. I had been trying to get him to go to counseling, mostly because he just wouldn't talk to me about how he felt or what was going on inside his head. So when I heard the news about Kevin, I thought it would be another log on the fire. My biggest concern became helping Alec maintain some kind of emotional balance. I worried that this would push him over the edge.

"You okay?" I asked him again.

"Yeah. I don't really want to talk about it," he said.

Typical Alec, I thought.

Soon, he fell asleep. I sat there for a long time, watching him. I wondered what he dreamed about. I wondered what was going on inside his head.

From very early on, he had seemed different from my other children – so much about him was difficult. I was a young parent, and in an attempt to figure out how to deal with Alec in a productive way, I read a lot about discipline. Nothing worked with him.

One of the tools I tried was "1-2-3 Magic." When he started misbehaving, he had until the count of three to change his behavior. It had worked great for my daughter – whenever I got to the number two she started to cry because she didn't want to go into timeout. But when I tried it on Alec (he was three or four), he finished the count for me, then stared defiantly.

In spite of his anger and behavioral issues, he was a good kid, and I loved him so much. He wasn't always angry. He played soccer for a few years. We had Nerf dart battles in the house: it was a blast, we'd laugh and play for hours. Birthday parties, Christmas, Easter egg hunts: he experienced all the typical carefree days of childhood.

I took him and the other kids to this pay-per-fish place, and I can still see his face when his line started to dance in the water. He enjoyed practicing martial arts, and I think that gave him something to focus on. He showed a more sensitive side with animals, particularly Lynn's dog Opus, a 185-pound mastiff. He outweighed Alec but, in spite of his size, Alec enjoyed playing with him. He'd chase Opus from the kitchen down the hallway into the front room and through the dining room, then turn around for Opus to chase him back into the kitchen. The game often ended with Alec laying on the kitchen floor with his head propped on Opus's belly.

But in recent years, he definitely seemed on edge. I hoped the death of his friend wouldn't make things worse.

3

Noises in the Night

My ex-wife, Diane, arrived at our house after work, and she told Lynn and I what she knew. The details were limited. The investigation was in its infancy. Lots of people were scared and worried, and no one knew what to think. Alec and Amy eventually went home with her, leaving Lynn and I to speculate, but we didn't have to wonder for very long. Details emerged as the day went on.

We learned that the Haines' daughter, their oldest child, was home the night the murders took place. Somehow during the attack, she had escaped to a neighbor's house, where she called for help. The feeling of safety and tranquility, normally present in our suburban neighborhood, was shattered as we thought about how terrifying that must have been for her. The comfort I usually found in those quiet streets turned to a sense of ominous foreboding.

Where was the person who had committed this terrible crime?

I wanted to support my three children as much as possible, so later that day I called them.

"You guys want to go with Lynn and me to church tomorrow?" I asked.

My daughter said she had to work, but Alec accepted the invitation. This surprised both of us. We had been trying to convince him to go to church with us for the past year, but he had always resisted. I had tried to be patient; after all, I had voiced the same objections for many years, and it had taken me a long time to find my way. I wanted to give Alec the same space I had needed, but I also wanted him to encounter the hope that I had found in my faith.

A stronger faith could get him through this tough phase of life, I thought to myself.

Sunday morning arrived, and Lynn and I picked up Alec from his mother's house. It was Mother's Day, a fact that added even more significance and tragedy to what had occurred the day before. I found my mind drawn to the Haines family again and again, especially the surviving daughter. What was she doing that morning? How could she even begin to cope with such a tremendous loss?

We arrived at our church and made our way inside. Alec decided to go with Lynn and me into the main service instead of going with the youth who met down stairs. This surprised me a little: the church had a very large youth group, and I thought Alec would want to hang out with kids his own age. There was a good chance he might see some classmates from school.

We found our way to the sanctuary with its stadium seating and balcony area. We sat on the right side of the main level closer to the back row. Lynn sat between the two of us. Alec's leg shook during the entire service, but that wasn't unusual for him: in environments where he was unfamiliar, he became nervous or high-strung, and this was a side effect. I didn't know if he was paying attention, but I hoped he was because it was a great sermon.

I'll never forget the message that day: "Submission." The pastor emphasized how we need to submit all of our problems and troubles to God.

"He forgives everyone and can relieve us of our pains and sorrows if we will just lay them down. Give them up to Him."

The sermon seemed to be reaching Alec; he was very attentive. I hoped he could forgive whoever had done this to Kevin and his parents. I didn't want the murders to turn him into a bitter, distrusting person. Perhaps he would also give God the rest of the things that weighed him down.

After church, we went for lunch at the restaurant where Amy worked as a waitress. We asked to be seated at one of her tables, and she lit up when she saw us. She seemed much better than the day before. I think staying busy at work helped, and she enjoyed her job. During lunch we let ourselves escape reality for a moment, engaging in fun conversation and laughing together.

The church service had helped Alec, or at least that's how it appeared to me. He looked relieved, less weighed down by Kevin's death, and more conversational than usual.

Maybe a stronger faith will help him.

After lunch, Lynn and I walked around the mall with Alec.

"Did you remember this is Mother's Day?" she asked Alec.

"Oh shoot, I forgot!" he said.

"You want to get your mother a card or something?" I asked.

"Good idea," he said, looking for the closest card shop.

He picked out a beautiful card.

"Cards are expensive," he complained, looking at the price on the back.

This was typical of Alec, always money-conscience. He spent his money so carefully, always had, even when he was a little kid with a dollar. I smiled when I heard him say that, but I let him pay for the card himself.

We dropped him off at his mother's house and went home, feeling a slight lift from lunch and shopping, a welcome distraction. Everyone seemed to be doing a little better.

Later in the afternoon, the boys came home: it was my week to have them at the house. Ever since the divorce, they had spent half of their time at my home and the other half at their mother's, switching houses week by week. At about four o'clock, they came bursting through the door with all of their gear, backpacks, and duffle bags. Alec toted his guitar back and forth in those days. He usually carried three or four bags, but Drew traveled pretty light. I tried to have supper for them soon after they arrived, and then they'd vanish somewhere in the house. I let them have that time to settle in because of the change in environment.

On some Sunday nights, we played cards or board games together, if they were in the mood for it, but most of the time they were in the basement playing video games or on the computer. They got along pretty well, as far as brothers go. But something about their interaction had always concerned me, and I'm not talking about their occasional fights. All brothers fight and wrestle, right?

What got my attention was the level of anger that Alec would often show. It alarmed me. Sometimes in the past, he would get so mad that he'd be on top of Drew, almost choking him. He didn't actually hurt him, but sometimes he got so angry that I wondered if he didn't want to.

And it wasn't just his brother who agitated him.

The sound of people chewing their food drove Alec into a rage, so much so that sometimes he had to leave the room. That was another point of contention between him and his brother, and one night before dinner, just to make a point, I put earplugs beside his plate.

"What are these for?" he asked, then realized what they were. "Oh, I get it. Very funny." But he wore them, and it helped.

Lynn didn't have children, so she asked a few school counselors and teachers she knew if Alec's behavior was common for a boy his age. The answer was always the same.

"No, it's not normal," they would say. "Or at least it's not common."

After his mother and I divorced and Alec still wasn't growing out of his anger, it had seemed like a great time to get him into counseling. We could use our separation as the reason, but my real motivation had been to get someone else's feedback on his extreme anger – he almost seemed to lose rational thought for minutes at a time, something that came out of nowhere and then vanished in a wave of tears and emotion.

Alec took medication for a few months, but he didn't like how it made him feel. Even at his age, he realized the medication lowered his awareness and ability to think quickly. So, I had told him that if he could keep his anger in check he could stay off the meds. Ever since then, he had seemed better. The number of outbursts diminished, but there were still very challenging moments when his anger boiled over. In hindsight, I realized that the anger never went away – I think he just figured out how to hide it.

I often wonder about the treatment options available to most people these days, especially children. So much effort went into helping Alec control his anger, but there was so little attention directed at discovering the root of it. What caused it? That seems to me to be the more important question.

"So how are you feeling?" I asked him for the twentieth time that Sunday night.

Alec's mind worked in a logical, analytical way, and I could tell he was trying to process and deal with things on that level. He always kept his feelings and emotions well below the surface.

"I'm okay, Dad, seriously. I'm fine."

The phone rang later that evening, maybe about 7:00pm. Lynn and I were sitting out in the living room, and I got up and answered it.

"Hello?"

"Hello, this is the Manheim Township Police. We have a few questions for Alec Kreider."

I had been expecting the police to contact Alec. After all, he was one of Kevin's two or three best friends – I assumed they'd want to talk to him about who could have done it and why. Alec spent a long time on the phone with the officer, but I didn't catch most of the conversation: he carried the phone into the kitchen, and Lynn and I stayed in the front room.

After the call, he seemed emotionally drained. All the happiness and relaxation from earlier in the day vanished. But, once again, these ups and downs seemed completely normal – he had just lost one of his best friends in a horrible fashion and was now being asked to revisit all the details of their friendship and tell everything he knew about Kevin. My heart ached for Alec and for the Haines family.

Lynn left after the call. Alec didn't want to chat about it, and he headed up to his room where he tended to spend a lot of time even though he didn't have a cell phone, computer, video game, or television up there. I often heard him practicing his martial arts, and when I asked him why he spent so much time in his room alone, he said he liked to think about things and get away from people.

So it didn't surprise me when Alec escaped to his room. He had a lot to think about. I just wished he would talk to me about what he was thinking! I stayed downstairs, the recent tragedy running over and over through my mind. Nothing was taken. No apparent motive.

Plus, it happened in the safety of their home. I couldn't help but glance at my windows and doors, mentally reminding myself to lock up that night. So many things about the situation unnerved me: the fact that it had happened in our town, to a wonderful family, for no apparent reason, in their home, and in the middle of the night. If it could happen to them, it could happen to anyone. A feeling of vulnerability shot through me.

None of it made any sense. That night I checked on Drew and Alec and made sure to lock all of the doors and windows.

Monday morning arrived. No one had slept well. I didn't want to send the boys to school, but I thought getting back into a routine would be good, so I sent them anyway. I knew things at high school would be crazy for Alec – everyone knew that Kevin was a close friend of his, and I worried about the additional stress and pressure this might cause him. He already struggled socially and emotionally.

At my own work, things were fairly normal. Everyone talked about what had happened, but I kept my head down and avoided conversations. I didn't want to talk about it, and I didn't want people to know how closely this had impacted my family. Yet, I couldn't avoid hearing things.

The Haines family had been stabbed to death. We all cringed at the horror of that thought – what a brutal way for someone to die. How could something so barbaric happen right here in one of our neighborhoods? What about those who committed the crime? How long would they walk around, free?

I didn't want the boys to be home alone when they returned from school, so I headed out early.

"How was your day, Alec?" I asked when he got home.

"It was okay," he said shrugging.

"Really?"

"I got emotional a few times," he admitted. "But for the most part, I held it together."

I could tell he didn't want to engage in a long conversation about his day at school. It was obvious he was drained from all the emotion. I left him alone but was determined to keep an eye on him.

The focus began to shift early that week from grief and shock to fear, anger, and speculation. Everyone in the community became involved in trying to find the killer. Or killers. The story dominated the local headlines. And there was confusion – no sign of forced entry? No sign of anything being taken from the home?

I thought back over the scene, how the Haines' daughter had come home early from college. She woke up in the middle of the night, heard sounds, and went over to her parents' room. She found her mother, who told her to run for help, but said nothing else. How could this be? The Haines' daughter didn't see anyone and escaped safely. The whole scene made no sense.

The Haines family had been killed with a knife – how could one person have done this to three people? Was there more than one person involved? One of the township officers told my daughter that this particular murder scene was the most brutal he had ever seen. Having known the family, I often wondered about their last moments – what sort of fear and terror had they experienced? How could that young girl cope with losing her entire immediate family? Lynn and I constantly prayed for her.

A few people at work knew of my connection to the Haines family, and they started asking me if I knew any additional details or insight, but I had nothing for them. I only knew what the newspapers reported. I couldn't blame people for asking – everyone wanted to know more. Everyone wanted to find out something in the hopes of feeling safe. But that information just wasn't out there. And if the Haines family hadn't been safe, how could any of us be?

Every night that week, I walked around the inside of my house checking all of the doors and windows to make sure they were locked. I had never done this before, but suddenly I felt unsafe in my own home.

One night the following week, when the boys were at Diane's house and I was home alone, I heard a noise. Usually my boxer Knock Out gave me some added security, but he was over at Lynn's house. I lay there quietly, for a long time, listening. My heart pounded.

There isn't anyone there, I told myself. *Calm down. You didn't hear anything.*
Another sound.
No, wait. What was that?
My mind raced.

There was an anxiety in my heart that I couldn't shake. No matter how often I told myself I was being stupid, there were feelings of fear, insecurity, and vulnerability at levels that I had never experienced before. Finally, I got up and walked across the room.

I locked my bedroom door.

So stupid, I thought to myself. *I shouldn't have to lock my own bedroom door to feel safe. It's silly. I'm being paranoid.*

Finally, behind all of my locked windows and doors, I fell asleep. And I wasn't alone in these feelings. In talking to my co-workers and neighbors, it became apparent that everyone felt the way I did. Everyone heard bumps in the night. Everyone locked their doors and windows. As a community, we no longer felt safe.

4

Here Comes the Sun

The first week passed with no indication of any leads, just a lot of speculation and rumor. With each passing day, it started to feel like this case would not be solved quickly: the authorities were talking to everyone, anyone, looking at all kinds of different options. At one point the state police even interviewed Alec in person, this time coming to our house.

The two officers came inside. It was a Sunday morning; we were just ready to leave for church. Lynn left, and I stayed behind with Alec. I sat on the arm of the couch listening to the questions. I wanted to make sure Alec was okay, that the officers weren't inappropriate in their approach, but I found myself paying close attention to how he reacted. I just couldn't shake the fear that Kevin's death might be the last straw for Alec's mental health.

The police officers maintained a very professional demeanor while also exhibiting some sensitivity to the fact that they were dealing with a sixteen-year-old boy who had just lost his friend. They certainly didn't treat Alec with kid gloves, but they were patient and low-key and casual. It wasn't a high-pressure interrogation.

"Did Kevin have any issues with anyone at school?"

"Was he involved with people online?"

"Did his sister have any boyfriends that might have had something against the family?"

"What do you guys do when you're on the Internet?"

Their questions jumped all over the place. One thought remained in my mind as I shook each police officer by the hand and they walked out the door: *Man, they still don't have any good leads. When are they going to find out who did this?*

One week after the murders took place, I found myself talking with Alec.

"The memorial service is tomorrow, Alec."

"I know," he said quietly.

"Lynn and I are going," I said. "Your brother, too. Do you want to come with us?"

"I really don't feel like going," he said.

"Look, Alec," I said, sitting down beside him, "I know this will be an emotional experience for you, but Kevin was one of your best friends. You need to go if only to show your respect and support for their family. They've always been good to you. It's the right thing to do."

Eventually, he agreed.

Saturday morning arrived. It was the kind of May morning that would normally feel crisp and fresh, but, knowing what was to come, I had a sense of lingering gloom. Lynn, Alec, Drew, and I planned on attending the service together. The house felt quiet, in spite of everyone showering, getting dressed, and eating breakfast.

"Which tie should I wear, Dad?" Alec asked me.

I helped him pick one out. He seemed particularly concerned with how he was dressed and wanted to give off the proper impression.

I didn't know exactly where to find the Otterbein United Methodist church, so we drove around Lancaster City for a few minutes until we passed by the church, eventually parking a few blocks away. As we walked along the broad street, the smell of spring all around us, I remembered something Kevin Haines had once told me.

"My grandmother helped start this church," he had said, obviously proud of the fact. How tragic that the church his grandparent had helped start was now hosting such a somber event for the family.

We walked into the large, stone building, and it was warm inside (There was no air conditioning.). A center aisle went all the way to the front, and long pews spanned each side of the church. By then, every space in the pews was taken (except for the front third, reserved for family), and ushers began filling the rear of the sanctuary with folding chairs. We waited in the vestibule while extra seating was put in place and thought we might end up standing for the service.

In spite of the number of people, the place stayed quiet. A lot of people moved around, finding seats and setting up chairs, but the busy atmosphere only made the silence more obvious. If anyone made any sound, it was quickly absorbed into the heights of the sanctuary.

"Do you guys need some help?" I asked the men setting up. They directed me to a room in the basement where I could grab some extra folding chairs. The downstairs hallway was isolated and empty, and its peace and tranquility felt a million miles away from the movement and sadness upstairs. I grabbed a few chairs and went back up.

By the time I got there, the entire place was packed, every new chair filled, and every bit of wall space lined with standing people. I found Lynn and Drew – they had saved a seat for me. But as I sat down, I realized that the parents of Alec's other best friend were sitting right behind us.

"How is your son doing?" I asked the mother. "This must be just as difficult for him as it is for Alec."

"I think he's doing okay. But he doesn't say much. I think he's just trying to get through each day."

"He can come over to our house any time," I said. "It might help Alec, too, you know?"

Meanwhile, Alec sat with his German teacher and the rest of his classmates, a few rows in front of me and slightly to the left. Kevin and Alec had been in German class together, and both of them had looked forward to going to Germany in the summer. Such a huge event, now only an afterthought.

At least I can keep an eye on him, I thought, but as I watched him, I became concerned. All around him, people struggled to maintain their composure. His teacher and his fellow students all looked emotional and sad, but Alec had a stoic look, as if he were trying to hold his emotions in. Alec was always very private, but I wished he would let some of it out.

How would Kevin's death affect him in the long run? I wondered.

The entire crowd hushed as the Haines family and relatives entered the sanctuary: brothers, sisters, cousins, aunts, uncles, parents, and grandparents filed into the church. They filled up the entire front section. There was this palpable feeling of sadness that accompanied them, like the approach of heavy, gray clouds. But they also exuded a sense of resilience.

The service reinforced this, as the family displayed compassion, grace, and faith throughout the morning. No one would have blamed them for being angry or lashing out, but each person who spoke demonstrated strength and even kindness. The themes of the day seemed to be love, forgiveness, and hope.

In between speakers, the church was mostly silent, except for the sister of Alec's other best friend sitting behind us. She had been close to all three boys, and during the service, the sound of her cries and sobs carried through the church. If everything else grew quiet, I could hear the sound of her sadness, echoing throughout the church, reverberating off of the stone walls. Her anguish resonated with everyone – she was letting out what the rest of us were so desperately holding in.

The most poignant part of the service came when Kevin's uncle, Lisa's brother, first spoke about Kevin, then made an emotional plea to the audience.

"If the person who did this is here, we would like to ask the person or persons responsible for this to come forward and admit what they've done."

So they think it's someone close to the family, I thought to myself. The oxygen left the room. It was a sobering thought. I looked over the crowd, wondering who among us might be a killer. Everyone sat completely still, waiting for the responsible person to stand up.

Later, he addressed the crowd again.

"The person responsible for this crime is probably in this room. If that is the case, do the right thing. Come forward."

The irony of this situation still haunts me.

The service ended, and we waited for the Haines family to stand up and leave. But as we waited, a lone voice rose out of the crowd: a gentleman, singing. I couldn't see him, but his voice overflowed with compassion. It felt like he was reaching out to me.

He sang through the entire Beatles' song, "Here Comes the Sun". The words spoke of hope and a sunshine, and I often thought about the song as I went through my own time of darkness in the following weeks.

Every time I heard those lyrics after that, I felt conflicting emotions of anger and hope: anger about what had been done to the Haines family. How could it ever be all right? Yet, there was hope – I had to believe that the sun would shine on us again.

The pastor stood up after the Haines family left the church.

"There are some counselors here for students to speak with if they'd like to hang around. They'll be up here around the front."

I felt emotionally drained, ready to leave, but I thought it would be a good idea for Alec to stay with his classmates. At first, he wasn't interested, but as students filed toward the front, he decided to join them. Lynn, Drew, and I walked outside – I was glad to see Alec had decided to stay. I thought he might need some private time.

We stood around outside the church, talking with other parents. A man with a TV camera positioned himself on the corner opposite the church, approaching people and trying to ask them questions, but everyone ignored him.

Really? I thought to myself. *Can't the media just leave this family alone?*

Soon, we saw signs that the students were finished inside.

"I'm going to go back in and try to find Alec," I told Lynn.

As I walked towards the church, I saw a bracelet lying on the church steps. It looked familiar, so I bent over and picked it up. It was Lynn's bracelet, a gift I had given her our first Christmas together, with the words of *Philippians 4:13* engraved on it.

I can do all things through Christ who strengthens me.

I stared at it for a moment, amazed that I had found it there – Lynn hadn't even realized that it had slipped off. The beauty and relevance of that verse hit home. *All things,* I thought. Then, I walked the rest of the way into the church.

I found Alec with his other best friend and his friend's older brother. Alec looked very upset and ready to leave, so we said our good-byes and started walking to the car. I felt a certain sense of relief: the service was over, and Alec had done okay. Perhaps we could move on, and Alec could get through this.

Then Alec stormed off, walking far in front of us. His arms were tense and straight and moved rigidly back and forth at his side. He looked up quickly and at times thrust his shoulders and head up, as if some inner agony was fighting to take over. Several times, he threw his clenched fist into the air.

This was the angry side to my son that was so painful for me to see.

He reached the car long before we did. By the time we got there, he was spent, tired.

"Talk to me, Alec. What are you feeling?" I asked him once we were in the car.

"I'm frustrated. I don't know what to do for my friends. They're so sad."

"That makes you feel angry?"

"No! I'm angry with those insincere hypocrites who were never nice to Kevin – now they're all upset! I don't get it."

As he sat there talking about the "hypocrites" at Kevin's memorial service, his anger and indignation intensified.

Then, he was finished. He didn't want to talk about it anymore. Even though he didn't say much, I was encouraged that he actually said something. It wasn't a lot, but it was a start.

I looked at Lynn out of the corner of my eye, and she reached over and squeezed my hand.

"Didn't that give you chills when Kevin's uncle asked the person responsible to come forward?" she asked me. For a second, I felt the same wave of emotion roll over me that I had felt when he made that plea from the front of the church.

"Can you imagine if that person was sitting there? How could you not stand up?" I asked her.

5

The Storm Arrives

Not much changed over the next few weeks.

Additional speculation and rumor swirled through the community, along with more visits to our home by the authorities, whose broad lines of questioning made it apparent that they still had no solid leads. This was disheartening, and the local residents became frustrated that nothing new was being discovered.

Eventually, word got out that a $25,000 reward was being offered to anyone with information in connection to the Haines case. It didn't surprise us – it just reinforced the fact that there were no new leads. I thought that if that kind of money was being offered, the investigators must still be lost, and it didn't give us much confidence that the killer would be caught anytime soon.

The boys stayed with their mother for the week after the funeral; then they came back to stay with me for their regularly scheduled week. Alec was quiet, as usual.

"How are you coping?" I would ask him. He said he didn't know how to act or feel. The entire community dealt with that confusion. I kept watching him closely for any signs of a worsening mood or a change in behavior.

But most of the signs I saw were encouraging: he attended a party with some new friends, talked more about his interest in girls, and started to reach out and pursue new relationships. He called me one evening and asked where he could buy flowers – three girls had befriended him and made it their goal to cheer him up. He wanted to show them that he appreciated their friendship.

This is new, I thought.

One Saturday, a few weeks after the funeral, Alec asked me a surprising question.

"Can I plant the flowers from my science project in one of our flower beds?"

"That's a great idea, Alec."

I watched him through the window as he carefully and gently took each of the flowers out of its current container and replanted them. I had to smile, watching the care and attention he put into the task.

He is moving on, I thought. *He'll be okay.*

Finally, the most encouraging sign of all: he agreed to talk to a professional counselor about what had happened to Kevin and also about the other things that bothered him and filled him with rage. I scheduled the appointment for the following Friday.

Finally, he can start on a path towards healing.

He and Drew returned to their mother's house on Sunday night.

But Alec would never make it to that counseling appointment. The storm I had seen for so long, brewing just under Alec's surface, was about to be unleashed on all of us.

Wednesday morning, June 6th: over three weeks had passed since the crime, something I thought about every night as I locked my doors. Since so much time had passed, I guess some of the edge had left us, but there was still a sense of dread or fear that jumped to the forefront as soon as anything out of the ordinary happened. And there was sadness for the Haines family. Always sadness.

I remember the police caught someone breaking into a local home during those weeks after the murders. When it first hit the news, everyone wondered if he was the killer. The police had responded quickly and aggressively to the call, and for a brief time, it took on a life of its own. Rumors flew, and everyone hoped this was a break in the Haines case. The response by the police and the reaction by the public demonstrated how easily we could now be sent into a state of alarm. After further investigation, it became apparent he wasn't involved – he had broken in looking for money or something, but the authorities were sure that he had not been involved in the crime we cared the most about. So the waiting continued.

I arrived at work that morning and looked at my cell phone, which showed that I had messages.

"Stupid phone," I muttered. I had been awake since 5:30am and had checked my phone a few times, but no messages had shown up. Oh well. I played my voice mail.

My daughter's voice, frantic and panicking, filled my head as I listened to the first message. My eyes grew wide. She had called in the middle of the night. I couldn't understand everything she said, but I got the point. Apparently Alec had threatened to kill himself the night before, and the police were called. I couldn't believe what I was hearing.

I thought my worst fears were coming true.

The second message was from Alec's mother. Her voicemail filled me in on some of the details. Alec had been on the phone with a girl friend, talking about killing himself; he had a gun (why did he have a gun? where did he get a gun?); and the police had been called to the house. They took him to Lancaster General Hospital, and from there he was sent to Philhaven, a mental health hospital in Mount Gretna, Pennsylvania.

That's all I knew, and it made me frantic. Obviously Kevin's loss had weighed heavily on him, and now, after years of struggling with his own issues, it had all boiled over, just as I had dreaded. My only concern at that point became getting to Philhaven as quickly as possible.

I called Alec's mother on her cell phone.

Nothing.

Where was she? I couldn't believe I wasn't able to reach her. Then, I started looking for information on Philhaven: telephone numbers or an address. Anything. But information that I would normally find in seconds evaded me, probably because of how frantic I became. As the minutes passed, I felt more and more distressed – I couldn't find what I wanted to find, and I couldn't get on the road to find my son.

It should be just a simple computer search, I mumbled to myself. *Why can't I find the phone number or address? This is ridiculous!*

Finally, it appeared, almost out of nowhere. What had taken me so long? I asked three questions in quick succession when I called.

"Hello, is this Philhaven?"

"Has Alec Kreider been admitted there?"

"What do I need to do to see him?"

I let my boss know what was going on, grabbed my things, and bolted for my motorcycle.

All I could think about was getting there as soon as possible.

He needs me. What if they move him somewhere else? What if they don't let me see him?

The urgency I had felt while searching for the information to contact Philhaven magnified as soon as I sat on my motorcycle. I took off, riding recklessly. It was easy to be out of control on the first part of my trip. I was on a two-lane, major highway and limited only by the speed of my motorcycle and my willingness to push myself faster and faster.

But I soon found myself on a congested, single-lane road. I knew the area well and realized I'd have a difficult time getting around traffic. I tailgated the car in front of me, looking for any opportunity to pass. The slower pace must have given me a moment to reflect on what I was doing and the stupidity of my riding.

I pulled off the road and stopped on a gravel drive for a moment, frightened at how carelessly I was riding. It wouldn't do Alec any good if I killed myself on the way. I removed my helmet, took a deep breath, and decided to check my phone for any messages. There were none. I took another deep breath, told myself to relax, and started off again.

Finally, I saw the road that led to Philhaven. I turned left and put it on full throttle down the country road. I flew past the lane and nearly locked up the brakes because of my urgency of purpose and agitation at missing the entrance. I made a U-turn, leaned left into the grounds, and followed the road around to the front of the main building. It sat just along the edge of some woods, a huge facility up on a hill. The 45-minute ride felt like it had taken me hours.

I walked in and saw the receptionist's desk off to the left-hand side. I checked in at around 9:00am, nearly an hour and a half since I listened to the first message on my phone.

"He's on the 2nd floor," the lady at the desk said, "in the juvenile ward."

I walked up the steps to the next level and made a left. I saw a sign outside the juvenile ward asking me to put all of my belongings into a locker.

That's why I couldn't reach Diane, I realized.

I used a telephone on the wall to call a staff member and explain who I was and why I was there. I waited. And waited. The juvenile ward itself was more secure than I had imagined. It was strange, thinking that Alec was locked inside there. Eventually I would come to appreciate that security – all of the kids in there struggled with something, and they needed close attention and supervision.

What was taking them so long? Where were they?

Finally, someone let me through the door. I walked back a hallway, passing a counseling room on the right and a few small offices on the left, then entered an open area. It was kind of like arriving at a town square: a few tables were scattered around, and a few benches lined the walls. I saw a glass conference room in one of the corners. I later found out that Alec's room was off to the left.

I found Diane. She was speaking with a lady.

"Hi, I'm Tim, Alec's father," I said, walking up to them, feeling breathless.

"Hi, I'm Alec's case manager," she explained. "I'm your contact for any questions you might have during Alec's stay at Philhaven. Alec is currently meeting with one of the lead psychiatrists here and is under evaluation. This doctor is excellent – Alec is fortunate he is on duty today."

I nodded.

"Now," she said, "I've got a few questions for the two of you."

She proceeded with a brief interview.

I answered her questions, but all I wanted was to find out why Alec was there. What could he have done to get himself in this situation? I had gone to bed the night before with a few concerns about my son and woke up the next morning to find out he'd been committed to a mental health facility. After ten minutes or so, his case manager finished the interview with us and walked away.

"What happened?" I asked, turning to Alec's mother.

Alec had been on the phone in his room with the door closed, talking to a girl. The girl's mother realized, by the way her daughter was responding and the answers she was giving, that Alec was making some disturbing statements: he was alone in his room with a gun, was in a very depressed frame of mind, and even made references to killing himself.

Since the girl's mother couldn't use the landline, she decided to drive to Alec's mother's house and alert her to what was taking place. My daughter heard what was going on and got very nervous. She decided to park herself outside of Alec's bedroom door to listen in. Then she heard a loud click, the chamber action on the gun – she believed that Alec had loaded a bullet, and she ran from the house, not wanting to hear it if Alec shot himself.

Meanwhile, Alec's mother didn't know what to do. How would Alec respond if she confronted him? Would he hurt himself? She called the police. They showed up with a crisis negotiator and several officers in full body armor. They listened in on Alec's friend's side of the conversation, and she repeated things that Alec said so that the police could try to determine the situation.

Alec continued talking to his friend, oblivious to everything going on only a few steps from his room. His friend kept chatting to him, keeping him on the phone, showing maturity beyond her years. She tried to say things that would get him to go outside of his room and downstairs.

"I'm kind of hungry. Are you hungry, Alec?" she asked.

"I sure could go for a glass of water," she said, trying to get him to do the same.

"You should grab something to eat," she suggested.

Eventually, she said something that convinced him to leave his room.

Meanwhile, monitoring the conversation, the officers knew Alec was on his way out. They got ready, and as Alec came out of his room and down the stairs, the officers burst into the house, pushed him to the ground and handcuffed him. The gun remained in his bedroom. No one got hurt.

The police led him outside, still handcuffed, past his mother and his sister. Neither of them had much of a chance to speak to him before he was directed into a waiting police cruiser and driven to Lancaster General Hospital.

"Alec looked so detached," his mother whispered to me. "He wasn't showing any emotion, and the look on his face was so empty. I've never seen him like that before."

Under those circumstances, he underwent a preliminary psychiatric evaluation. While at the hospital, his mood swung irrationally, from a place of calmness, to despondency, to anger. Occasionally, he became completely irrational. The doctors determined that he was far too unstable for them to treat there, so they sent him to Philhaven for a more thorough evaluation.

"I've never seen him like this before," Diane said. She sounded frightened. "He hasn't slept for days. What do you think's wrong?"

I could only shake my head. My mind felt overwhelmed with its own questions.

Why would he threaten to kill himself?

Was there any way we could get him the kind of help that would change the course of his life?

I didn't realize it at the time, but it was far too late for that.

6

The Password
Is "Broken Window"

I looked into the evaluation room where a doctor questioned Alec. It was a small room with windows around the two exterior walls. I desperately wanted to be in there. Alec's back was toward me. For a moment, I remembered him as a little boy.

I pictured him as an eight or nine year old, and he was doing this little ballerina dance for his grandmother, twirling around the room. It was hard to imagine him doing something like that now – he had become so serious during his adolescence. He'd probably be embarrassed at the memory. But in that video, he was up on his toes, spinning, his arms up, and it was really cute. He was just playing around, entertaining his Nanny, acting silly.

Then another, more recent, memory: we were in the garage, and I was teaching him how to drive. He sat in the driver's seat, and I stood off to the side, behind the car.

"Put it in reverse," I told him as he got situated, put on his seat belt, and started the car.

"Put it in reverse," I reminded him again, and he nodded his head, but the reverse lights never came on. Instead, the car jerked forward and plowed into the riding lawn mower parked in front of the car!

"Whoa, whoa!" I shouted, kind of laughing. "You have to make sure it's in reverse!"

I ran around to the side of the car, but for some reason he just kept giving it gas, and he ran into the mower again, pushing it through the drywall.

I laughed about it, but he was mortified. He hated to mess up. He couldn't stand it when he did something wrong.

But that seemed like a long time ago. The doctor sat across from him, and I tried to read what was happening on the other side of the glass by the expression on his face. Was he troubled? Relieved? Unsettled? Frustrated? Alec's mother and I both waited, deep in our thoughts. I kept going over everything they had told me, trying to piece together what it would mean for Alec in the coming days, weeks, and months.

Finally, the evaluation ended. Alec came out of the room and walked over to us. We spoke with him briefly.

"How are you?" I asked.

"I'm okay," he said. "I want to go home."

He looked scared, exhausted, and disoriented. I hugged him.

"I love you," I said.

Then, they led him away, walking slowly down the hall, and Alec's doctor came up to us. He was probably in his late thirties with short black hair. As soon as he spoke, I could tell he was concerned.

"Can we speak for a few minutes about Alec?" the doctor asked us as Alec disappeared through a doorway. The doctor's voice held a weight to it, a heaviness. It struck me that whatever I had thought might be wrong with Alec, things were much more serious than that. Sometimes when doctors come out to talk to you about a patient, there's something in their voice that assures you the patient will be fine. There was none of that in this man's voice.

"Sure, what can we do for you?"

"I'm very alarmed for Alec," he said. "I'm worried that he might harm himself or someone else. One of the most helpful things we can receive from you right now would be as many details as you can recall about Alec. Nothing is insignificant. I'd like to hear any memories you have of him, his behavior, his thought processes, or anything that sticks out."

I had some issues with anger as a child, and I knew what it was like to have ugly thoughts, as most of us do. I think I had always hoped that Alec would grow out of it, like I had. I thought that perhaps Alec was dealing with typical teenage anger, but the doctor's demeanor made it obvious that it was way beyond that. Once again, the seriousness of the situation settled in as I searched my brain for anything about Alec that might be helpful.

"From very early on," I began, "Alec was different from my other children. He got angry faster. Discipline with him was very difficult. I don't know; we were young parents, so I did a lot of reading and trying to figure out how to discipline my children. But nothing worked with Alec."

Diane sat beside me, nodding.

"We tried timeouts, but sitting in timeout didn't matter to him. We tried rewards – he didn't really care about that. We tried taking things away from him, like the toys from his room. I remember one time that he got angry – he was probably around five years old, give or take – and we got into a disagreement. He refused to listen. 'I'm taking away this toy,' I told him. 'Fine,' he said. 'Okay, then I'll take this one, too.' 'Fine,' he said again. Before I knew it I had taken all of his toys, and he didn't even care."

I sat there in silence for a moment, reliving the incident, staring at the floor.

"I kept those toys for a month. A whole month. And he just didn't care. He never even asked for them back."

The doctor took some notes on his clipboard.

"It's not that he was always angry, but it seemed as if his intellectual maturity has always been well beyond his emotional maturity. I think that's what makes life difficult for him. He looks at life intellectually, sees everything that doesn't make sense, but can't process it emotionally or understand why the world isn't the way he thinks it should be; this leads to frustration and anger."

The doctor nodded, writing. Besides our conversation, the hospital was quiet. I wondered where they had taken Alec and what he was doing.

"Small things bother him a lot," I continued. "The sound of people's chewing and breathing really annoys him. This year, he seemed to have more difficulties than before. Headaches, fatigue. He feels down so much of the time and rarely seems truly happy. And I've tried to get him to talk to a counselor about it. I'm always trying to get him to open up, but I don't think he really shares honestly with anyone. Not me, not his mother, not his school advisors. But he's also been doing very well in school. I can't remember the last time he missed a day. He gets very good grades. I just don't know."

I felt like I was rambling. We tried to fill the doctor in on everything that came to mind about Alec. He asked a few questions about certain events or situations.

"Did it surprise you to discover he had threatened to commit suicide?" the doctor asked.

I looked over at Diane, then back at the doctor.

"No, I can't say that comes as a surprise," I said quietly.

That's a tough admission to make, and I paused for a moment before continuing.

"I know he's a troubled kid. I know he feels depressed a lot. I've been keeping a close eye on him. I thought if I loved him enough, watched him closely enough, I could get him through these difficult teen years."

At this point, I started getting emotional, so I stopped talking. Alec's mother took over, and my mind wandered through the events of the past month. I had begun seeing a few positive signs and had thought things might be changing for him. Now, was it too late? He was admitted to a mental health facility, admittedly in a terrible state of mind. What could I have done to avoid this?

The doctor stopped writing and looked up at us. I could tell he was trying to proceed with caution.

"I want to share my observations with you," he began, "but I have to warn you. I am concerned for your son. In fact, I am extremely worried about him."

His compassion and concern disarmed me and commanded my attention.

"Alec is having very dark, alarming, and sometimes suicidal and homicidal thoughts. He is suffering from depression and most likely has been, on some level, for a long time. At this point, it is my opinion that Alec poses a threat to himself and possibly others. Based on my evaluation, I am prescribing anti-psychotic medication and medicine which will offset the side affects of the anti-psychotic and an anti-depressant."

I closed my eyes and exhaled, leaning forward in my seat. This was devastating news. And alarming. *Suicidal and homicidal.* The doctor made a point of mentioning both, and the second one caught me off guard. Obviously, I expected the suicidal thoughts to come out – that's why we were there, because he had threatened to commit suicide. But homicidal thoughts?

"Alec hates medication," I said, shaking my head. "He won't even take aspirin for a headache. Are you sure these medications are necessary?"

"I am very concerned about Alec's state of mind," the doctor reiterated. "I only prescribe medication as a last resort. But Alec needs this right now."

"But why don't we at least try something else first? Can't we try medication down the road if nothing else works?"

"Mr. Kreider, I insist that Alec be given these medications. He could be in grave danger without them."

I sat back. What else could I do?

"I will not be Alec's treating physician. The staff will inform you of who will be responsible for Alec's care. They'll also walk you through the process of what's to come."

He shook our hands, turned, and walked away. We waited there a few minutes before Alec's case manager returned and began walking us through the day-to-day life of having a child in Philhaven.

"You can visit Alec any day from 4:00 to 8:00 PM. He can receive phone calls from only the two of you. The best time to call is just before lights out, which is between 9:00 and 9:30 PM. Alec's required daily activities may render him unavailable for phone calls during the day. What is a password that we can use to verify your identity over the phone and ensure he doesn't receive any unauthorized calls?"

I came up with a few lame suggestions. Then Diane offered an idea.

"Remember how Alec broke that window when he was little during a temper tantrum? Let's use 'broken window' as our password."

It was easy to remember and seemed appropriate for the situation we found ourselves in. The window was broken. Shards of glass were everywhere. Now, what would we do?

36

The morning passed quickly, and soon Diane had to leave for work. I stayed, trying to find out more about where we would go from there.

"Alec will be going through individual therapy sessions as well as family counseling sessions with you and his mother," the case manager explained. "Your other children will not be involved with the process at this time. The counselor will contact you regarding the times of the sessions."

I nodded, trying to store all the information somewhere in my brain, which felt overloaded and numb.

"Anything else?"

"I think that's all for now, Mr. Kreider. Do you have any more questions?"

"Yes."

She looked at me, waiting.

"Can I talk to Alec now?"

She paused for a moment. I could tell she was trying to think of the most tactful way of saying "no."

"Mr. Kreider, I would advise against that right now. He is in his room, and he's finally getting some rest. Perhaps, if you'd like, you could look in on him?"

I nodded and stood up. She gave me directions on how to get to his room, and I walked down the silent hallway, wondering so many things.

A young man sat outside of Alec's room.

"Hi, how's it going?" I asked him.

"Fine," he said, smiling.

"Is this Alec Kreider's room?"

"Yes, sir."

"I'm his father. I just want to look in on him if that's okay."

"Sure, go ahead."

I looked through the doorway in Alec's room. He was asleep with his back toward me, and I felt a small surge of relief at the fact that he could rest. The room was barren with a small cot and a nightstand with a light on it. The door to the bathroom was just beyond his bed. The room was dim, and all the lights were off.

As I stood there for a few minutes and watched him sleep, I couldn't help but wish there was some way to rewind the clock 24 hours, change things for the better, somehow keep him from this road he was on.

"So, what's the plan?" I asked the young man outside the door.

"Well, because of the concern regarding Alec, his door will be open 24-7. He'll be under constant visual supervision. He won't be able to do anything on his own: using the restroom, showering. Someone will be with him at all times."

He sounded compassionate and understanding, and I wondered what he thought about that job: watching someone's every move so that they would not hurt themselves or other people.

"He's not going to like that," I warned. "He's a modest kid – he doesn't even like it when I'm in the bathroom with him at home."

"We're committed to keeping him safe. It's the only way."

I looked in on Alec one more time. Still sleeping. I looked at my watch. I needed to get back to work. My job. That was the last thing I wanted to think about.

"Thanks," I said.

"No problem, Mr. Kreider. We'll take good care of your son."

As I road back to work, I couldn't stop thinking about Alec. He was far more disturbed than I ever could have imagined. It seemed like Kevin's death had pushed him over the edge.

7

"I Love You, Dad"

Later that same day, Diane and I drove to Philhaven for a scheduled visit with Alec. I wanted to go there with her so that he could see we were united in our desire to support him in spite of whatever past divisions our family had experienced.

Once in the juvenile ward, the hospital staff directed us to the same room Alec and the doctor had initially met in during his evaluation. We sat down at the small table and waited for the staff to bring Alec to us. I had no idea what to expect. What would Alec be feeling? Anger? Sadness? Depression? Peace?

When he first walked in, we each gave him a long hug. He wore normal clothes and looked tired. I could tell immediately that he was in a bad mood.

"I can't believe I have to stay here," he said, very agitated and angry. "This place is never going to help me."

His mother and I glanced at each other.

"Alec," I said, "this is the best place for you, at least until you level out. The doctors are concerned that you might hurt yourself."

"Yeah, well, if you want me to end things, keeping me here is one way to make sure it happens."

I froze. That was the first time I had ever heard him threaten to kill himself, and I didn't know how to process it or how to respond. But in spite of his harsh words, I could tell he was frightened at the situation. At that point, he had no control over his own life.

"This place is only making me more crazy," he continued, glancing wildly around the room. "I know what I'm going to do, the first chance I get. If you don't get me out of here, I'll do it. People following me around? Into the shower? Into the bathroom? This is ridiculous!"

I was heart-broken. I didn't know what to say, so I just sat there waiting for his rant to end.

"This place isn't helping. It's only making me worse," Alec said over and over again.

We tried to calm him. We tried to explain why the doctors needed to do what they were doing. I struggled to stay composed, listening to my 16-year-old son emphatically state that he was going to take his life the first chance he got. But seeing him that way helped me to understand, perhaps for the first time, just how serious the situation was.

Eventually we calmed him down, and as his anger and frustration began to evaporate, they were replaced by fear and anxiety. He put his head down on the table and began to sob.

"I just don't want to be here," he stammered amongst the cries. "I just want to be home."

I tried to comfort him.

"Right now, because of what happened, we don't have any options. This is the best place for you. I know you don't believe me, but it is. You'll just need to take some time and get better, and then you'll be ready to come home."

By the time we left, his condition had improved, but he was still scared and upset about having to spend the night there. We hugged him good-bye. My boy, the one I had taken care of for his entire life, was now in someone else's care. I felt helpless. He looked terrified, betrayed.

I feared for his life and his future.

As we left, his case manager reminded us of the upcoming family and individual counseling sessions on the schedule.

"His progress will be monitored, and a discharge date will be determined based on his progress."

"Who makes that decision?" I asked.

"The hospital doctors and the case manager."

We would have no input in when he got out.

"How long do you think he'll have to stay?" I asked.

"We anticipate a minimum stay of ten days, but it could go longer."

Ten days! How sick must he be if they wanted to keep him ten days! How would Alec handle that kind of news? How long would he have to be medicated? But I was tired of asking questions, so Diane and I walked outside and headed home.

It was 9:00pm, around twelve hours after I heard that first voicemail message from Diane. It was quiet in the house, and my mind kept recycling the events of the day. So much had changed. More things than I ever could have imagined.

I called Alec. They brought him to the phone, and hearing his voice broke my heart again. He was obviously upset, crying as he spoke.

"Dad, I just want to come home. Please, tell them to let me come home."

His sobs rocked me to the core. If there was any possibility of taking him out of that place, I would have driven up there and done it. But it was out of my hands. I encouraged him to pray and to try and stay positive.

When we finally hung up, I was emotionally and physically exhausted. Lynn was there, and we discussed the events of the day. I figured I should take my own advice, so we prayed: for Alec, that he would find strength and peace, that he would get better and come home soon; for us, that we would have the strength and wisdom we needed.

All of this in one day, I thought to myself. *I am exhausted.*

Unfortunately, I had no idea that this was just the beginning of an unimaginable journey for Alec, myself, and my family.

I couldn't sleep that night, but for once, it wasn't for fear of the killer still on the loose. I rolled over time and time again, stared at the ceiling, tossed and turned. In my head, I went over every detail of my conversations and visits with Alec, trying to find a positive sign, something on which to hang some hope. But no matter how I looked at the situation, it seemed so bleak.

I tried to put myself in his place, feel what he felt. He was alone in a strange place, being followed around wherever he went. Any semblance of privacy had been torn from him. He was obviously tormented, angry, and scared.

I don't remember sleeping that night, but I'm sure I did. At some point, the sun rose. *How is Alec doing?* I wondered. *When he wakes up this morning, what will be his state of mind?* My only concern at that point was for Alec, his mental health and his future.

But I had to go to work.

Once I arrived in the office Thursday morning, I could tell that word of Alec's situation had spread. I guess it's one of those whisper-down-the-lane things, where one person tells someone else who tells someone else. But it wasn't done in a mean spirit. My closest friends at work offered me a shoulder to lean on for support. I found reassurance there – so many people thought of and prayed for Alec and my family, and it gave me an immense feeling of comfort.

Philhaven was generous in regards to the visitation hours, but Diane and I were the only ones permitted to see him. Because of Alec's emotional state of mind, as well as our determination to support him, we visited every day. We decided to split up the time so that Alec had someone with him as much as possible. Occasionally, we visited at the same time, which worked out okay, but our goal became ensuring that at least one of us was there with him during his visiting hours – we saw ourselves as his only lifeline to the outside world.

I talked to my employer and rearranged my work schedule, going in early so that I could leave by 3:00 and be at Philhaven when visiting hours started. Everyone at my office understood and worked with me.

Those first two days were unbelievably difficult. Alec continued to sway back and forth from anger to frustration, from fear to hope, from hopelessness to calm. I began to realize that there was only one thing that I could focus on: trying to help him understand that I loved him and would be with him through anything he needed to face.

"I am your father," I told Alec many times in those days. "I love you and will always be here for you, no matter what."

No matter what.

Have you ever thought about those words, what they actually mean? Sometimes we say those words and have no idea what the "what" might someday be. Alec needed my strength as never before. His face filled with anguish and torment at the thought of staying in the hospital, yet I was powerless to help. I could do nothing but love him as he tried to obtain some sort of emotional restoration.

He will get better, I told myself. *Things will get better. This isn't permanent. Have faith and be strong.*

"I know you can do this," I told Alec, also encouraging him to pray.

The hospital staff told his mother and I that we could bring in snacks for him, and he'd be allowed to have them at various times throughout the day. We knew he would be there for at least ten days, so I stocked him up with candy bars and jumbo chocolate chip cookies, two of his favorites. Such a small thing, but I searched for any way to help him, no matter how trivial.

Our first scheduled family counseling session came on Thursday evening, something I eagerly anticipated. I hoped the session would give me a better idea of Alec's emotional state, as well as a clearer picture of what needed to be done for him. Alec, his mother, the therapist, and I all sat down around a small table in an office. It was kind of a cluttered room with books and files resting on cabinets and chairs.

Immediately, I sensed that Alec still experienced serious ups and downs. His voice took on an agitated tone, displayed an ever-present frustration with having to stay in the hospital. He came across as being tense and annoyed. I have a feeling that for those first few days he held this belief that if he continued to show them how upset and angry he was, they would give up and let him out. In fact, the opposite was true, something I tried to communicate to him.

"Nothing positive is going to come from this," he hissed. "It's humiliating, being watched 24/7. They won't let me do anything. I need to be at home. That's where I should be."

His mother and I sat there quietly while he vented.

"And these sessions are worthless. How is any of this going to help me?"

We took turns speaking to him, calming him down. After a few minutes, his emotions seemed to come down a few levels, and he began to show some signs of accepting his situation. This allowed the therapist to redirect the conversation.

"Alec," she asked, "what is bothering you? What are the issues as you see them?"

He paused.

Then he opened up, saying things that I had been trying to get him to share for years. He told us some of the thoughts, emotions, and struggles he had been going through. I couldn't believe it – I had reached out to him for such a long time, and while he always discussed surface level things that bothered him, he had never let me in any further.

He had often told me that he was having dark thoughts and that he fought to control them. Yet, he never told me exactly what they were. I had even shared with him the dark thoughts I had at his age in hopes that he would open up. He had asked me how I dealt with my own demons, and why I hadn't acted on them. I discussed breaking points, and how I got through them.

Still, he never gave me details on his thoughts. "You wouldn't understand," he'd say, or "I don't want to talk about it." During his brief stint with a psychologist – he had gone twice – nothing serious had ever emerged. Based on his sessions with Alec, the psychologist had said he did not see any issues of major concern.

But Alec had become increasingly adept at hiding his true thoughts and feelings. I was certain that Alec had not opened up with him or discussed any of the things that truly bothered him. This is why I had continued to encourage him to return to counseling as his demeanor became darker over the last few months.

Sitting there in that family counseling session at Philhaven, listening to Alec finally confess his true thoughts and feelings, it was obvious to me that Alec had never said any of these things to anyone before. So much had been hidden, and for a long time. Not just in the recent months or years, but for as long as he could remember.

"I feel like there are two sides to me," he said. "One side wants to do what's right and good, but the other side gets so angry and violent. I feel like they're fighting against each other all the time – sometimes when I look in the mirror, I can see it all happening. I can actually see my two selves battling."

This made some sense to me – I knew that Alec held honesty and integrity in high esteem. He was concerned with justice, sometimes to the point of rage. The deeper he went in explaining this dual nature, the more anguished and frustrated he sounded.

His thoughts were incredibly dark, depressing and horrible. The internal conflict he had experienced was intense. He couldn't explain why or where these nightmares came from. He described his efforts to fight them, to control them. He worked very hard to keep everything covered up. But as he told us these things and saw the disbelief on our faces, there was also some pride in his ability to maintain control, to keep his thoughts hidden.

"I guess I fooled everyone," he remarked, smirking. He had always felt intellectually superior to most people, and I think he took some pride in knowing that he had been successful in hiding his thoughts.

For the first time, I felt frightened. The frankness in his voice, the disconnection between what he was saying and what is normally acceptable, the absence of any regard for the emotions or welfare of others. For the first time, I received a glimpse into what he had always alluded to, and it terrified me.

I left the session overwhelmed with my own anxieties about Alec. He was in more trouble than I had known. Before that session, ten days sounded like a long time for him to be in Philhaven; as we left, I wondered if it would be long enough.

When I got home, I told Lynn about everything that Alec had said.

"He could be in there for a while, Lynn. He needs long-term care. This is serious."

I sat there, holding a glass of water. Lynn reached over and held my hand. I looked up at her, barely able to hold it together. She and I spoke a lot about the parenting decisions that I had made. Why hadn't I been more insistent in getting him help earlier? Did my attitude and flaws as a young father contribute to where Alec was today? It's a challenge parenting kids, and when they're only with you half the time, it is an even more difficult task. I began to question my worth as a father.

"I failed him. I failed my son."

"Tim! You know that's not true."

"But it is! I am his father. It is up to me to protect him, even from himself. I failed – I should have been more insistent about getting him into counseling. If I had only been stronger, he wouldn't be in this situation."

Lynn tried to dissuade me, but I couldn't get these thoughts out of my head: Alec's current situation was my fault. I had failed my son.

That evening, I called Alec to say good night.

"How are you, Alec?"

"I'm doing a little better."

A moment of silence.

"I tried praying," he said. "It helps."

Perhaps this will help Alec in other ways, I thought. *Maybe something good can come out of this.*

"Man, I can't wait to get back in my own bed," he said, then adding, "I really miss you guys. I miss home."

"It won't be long, Alec. Hang in there."

At the end of the conversation, we said good night.

"I love you," Alec said.

"I love you, too," I said.

I hung up and stared at the phone. I had been giving Alec hugs and telling him that I loved him since the day he was born. But he had never told me, "I love you." Not once. He guarded his emotions, rarely verbalized his feelings. Those three little words meant more to me than anything else he ever could have said.

Why did it take him so long to reach this point? I wondered. *I hope it's not too late for him.*

I told Lynn about the things that Alec said on the phone, and we both cried happy tears over what was happening. A light appeared in the darkness. In spite of the pain surrounding the situation, and the things that had been revealed about my son, I started to feel the slightest glimmer of hope – perhaps all of this had happened for a reason. Perhaps now Alec would get the help that he needed and find peace.

8

One Last Thing To Discuss

On Friday, I attended the hearing that would determine Alec's length of stay at Philhaven. Because his admittance was involuntary, they could not hold him for more than 72 hours without a hearing to determine the appropriate course of action. Alec's counsel was assigned to him. Philhaven's counsel attended, along with the supervising psychiatrist, the mediator, Alec, Diane, and me.

Alec entered the room escorted by two male staff members. He looked tired and very much like a little boy. The two staff members took positions against the wall behind the mediator and remained there throughout the hearing. As we began, it became obvious that the decision regarding Alec's stay had been determined before anyone entered the room.

His supervising psychiatrist was asked to give details about the circumstances resulting in Alec being admitted. She struggled to give a coherent and accurate account of the events, which frustrated me to no end. Her poor testimony was littered with inaccurate assumptions, something that concerned me more and more as the hearing went on. If they couldn't get Alec's story right, how could I be sure that proper attention was being paid to him?

"What is your opinion of Alec's condition, and should his stay be extended?" Philhaven's counsel asked her.

"I believe he is currently a danger to himself and requires additional treatment prior to being discharged."

Within minutes, the ruling was made.

"Alec Kreider's stay will be extended, not to exceed 21 days."

His discharge date remained at the discretion of the treating psychiatrist. Everything depended entirely on the progress made by Alec.

While I felt extreme disappointment when the ruling was made, I still knew that he needed major help. I agreed – he was a danger to himself, and the best place for him was probably right there until we figured something else out.

"How are you?" I asked him after the hearing.

He shrugged his shoulders.

"That lady couldn't get anything right," he said. "I can't stand my sessions with her – she doesn't have a clue."

Yet, he seemed more accepting of his fate than at any other time during his stay.

"You have to work with her, Alec. She has to see improvement and cooperation, or you won't be going anywhere."

"I know. But some of the stuff they have me doing during the day is pointless."

"Everything they do has a purpose. You need to do the stuff they ask you to do. Your behavior is being watched, and if you don't show signs of improvement, you'll have to stay."

"I know," he said. "I'll try to do better."

The weekend arrived, and along with it came extended visiting hours at the hospital. We played cards, chess, and hung out, talking about how he felt, how he was coping with things.

"How's the journal going?" I asked him. He was required to write one while at the hospital.

"I like it; it's cool. But I'm careful about what I write in it – I know they'll read it at some point."

"Write whatever you're thinking about. That's the only way they can help you. Plus, it might feel good to get some of those things out."

He nodded, smiled, and moved one of his pieces across the chessboard.

"I still don't get why I'm here. I don't understand what they can do for me."

I stared down at the board.

"Just follow the rules, Alec. Do what they ask you to do."

After I moved my piece, I looked up. He was looking around the room.

"Thanks for visiting me, Dad."

I followed his gaze. There were a lot of lonely people there, a lot of people who never got any visitors. I think Alec started to appreciate his blessings.

"So what's everyone saying about me out there?" he asked, moving one of his chess pieces. I studied the board

"Out where?"

"You know what I mean. At school. Everyone probably thinks I'm crazy."

"We're not telling anyone what's happening. You don't have to worry about it. When you get home, everything will be fine. And even if people do find out, they won't blame you for going through a tough time. Alec, your best friend was killed. Anyone else could have responded the same way."

He just nodded, watching my hand as I made my move.

"Plus," I said, "it's the beginning of the summer. By the time school starts in the fall, everyone will have forgotten you were away."

Later, the irony of these conversations would haunt me.

"So, Dad, do you think I could maybe talk to her on the phone sometime?"

He tried to ask in a nonchalant way, in the mean time sliding a piece across the board. He was referring to the girl with whom he had been speaking when the police were called to his house, the girl who somehow managed to get him out of the room before he hurt himself. The more he talked about her, the more obvious his infatuation became.

"No. Right now they say you can only speak to your mother and I."

Inside though, I started to worry. I remembered the emotion and adrenaline involved with my first crush. The wild swings, from a high "she loves me" to the depths of "she loves me not." I knew the havoc those feelings could bring about in a teenager with a more stable emotional state than Alec. What they would do to him worried me.

"That's so stupid. I really want to talk to her. She's a good friend, and I like her. She's nice. I don't know. Maybe you could talk to someone, see if I could call her?"

"Let's see how these sessions go, Alec. Maybe if you show signs of improvement, they'll give you a few privileges."

I moved a piece on the chessboard.

"Check mate," I said, smiling. He groaned.

On Sunday evening, that first weekend, our second family session took place. We met with a different counselor since Alec's normal counselor did not work on the weekend. Alec seemed more acclimated to the environment, and his mood was so much better.

The three of us had been informed of the possibility of his returning home at the end of the week.

"Dad, if I do get to come home, let's have a picnic or something. I'd like to see my friends again."

He was encouraged and upbeat by the news. I could tell he missed home and his brother and sister, who weren't allowed to come in to see him. We spent a fair amount of time planning out the details for the picnic because it seemed to help his spirits quite a bit. Because of all this, our session began on a good note. But Alec still wasn't happy about the one-on-one supervision.

"I'm not sure why these guys still have to come with me to the bathroom. To the shower. Everywhere. It's disgusting."

"Alec," the counselor said. "It's for your own protection."

"But there's no need for it! I don't feel that way any more. I'm working hard, trying to do what you ask. I just don't like being followed around all the time."

I jumped in.

"I've met the guys that are responsible for you, Alec, and they're good guys. They're reasonable. You're getting there. Hang in there. Just keep doing what you're doing."

"It's up to the treating psychiatrist," his counselor explained. "She still feels that it is a necessary precaution."

I could see Alec back away from that.

"But I don't even need to be here any more. I'm good. I can continue my treatment on my own, at home."

We finally convinced him to see the process through, and he gained an acceptance for his position by the end of the session. His response encouraged all of us. I saw improvement, and while I still appreciated the amount of work to be done, real progress was made.

A couple of the staff members led Alec back to his room, but his mother and I stayed behind to speak with the counselor.

"There's just one more thing we want to discuss with you, in private," I said.

"Sure, what's on your mind?"

"Diane and I both feel it's very important to address this before Alec leaves here. You see, he has feelings for the young lady he had been talking to on the phone the night the police came. He has very strong feelings for her."

The counselor nodded. I continued.

"She enjoys Alec's company and definitely considers him a good friend, but nothing more," I said.

"And you're worried about how Alec might respond when he finds this out?"

I nodded.

"Well," she suggested, "perhaps, if you want to, we could bring it up on Tuesday night when he meets with his regular therapist?"

We agreed, and I left Philhaven that night feeling up and then down: Alec had made huge progress in such a short time, and I thought he might be on the right track. Yet, I felt such strong trepidation about what his reaction would be to the news that this girl was not interested in him as anything more than a friend. How would he take the news? Would it set him back, wash away any of the progress he had made?

That was a physically and emotionally exhausting week. I didn't eat or sleep very much. My mind circled around to Alec, his situation, and how I could make it better so that it wouldn't destroy his future. By Monday morning, I began prepping myself for the Tuesday evening session.

If we can effectively work through Alec's feelings for this young lady, I thought to myself, *and perhaps redefine this relationship, he might not lose too much ground. He might be able to come home soon.*

9

The Confession

Tuesday morning, I checked a message on my cell phone.

"Hi Mr. Kreider, this is Alec's therapist. I've been speaking with Alec's treating psychiatrist, and she is not comfortable with Alec planning on returning home at the end of this week. We both still have serious reservations about Alec's stability and believe an intensive outpatient program might be the best thing for him once he is discharged from Philhaven. We're working on the schedule for this, but I'm not sure that we can work it out for him to begin that program until next week. We can talk more about it this evening at the family session."

Disappointment washed over me. I knew it would be a big blow to Alec as well: he couldn't wait to see his family and friends again. Couple that with the other potentially upsetting news we needed to cover with him that night, and it was with great weariness that I left the house for our family counseling session.

As had become usual, Alec's mother and I made the trip to Philhaven together. On the way, we discussed the news about him not being able to come home on Saturday. We were both disappointed and concerned about the affect this might have on Alec, and we strategized about the best way to break the news to him about his friend. We both felt the stress of knowing this was going to be a very important session for Alec on his road to recovery.

We walked into the very small counseling room, and the four of us got seated. Alec sat in a chair on the left side of the room, and his therapist sat on the right side of the room almost directly in front of Alec. I sat in a chair close to Alec, on his right side, and Diane sat next to me.

As it turned out, someone had already informed Alec that they had extended his stay. He seemed slightly down regarding the news, but I was surprised – compared to many instances during the previous week, he took it well. He seemed assured of a Monday or Tuesday release, and I think having an end date gave him something to set his sights on.

"If you keep cooperating with your psychiatrist and doing what these folks ask you to do, the rest of your stay here will only get easier," I said.

Alec was more upbeat than I had seen him for a long time, so I was cautiously optimistic about introducing the next topic of conversation: the feelings he had for the girl he had been talking to the night this all began.

Anyone who has had a "first love" knows how painful it is when the feelings are not reciprocated. It becomes a significant, emotional landmark in our lives, and, at the time, the rejection is difficult to deal with. We become infatuated with the person, thinking about them constantly – they become the focal point of our world, if only for a short time. This is what the girl represented for Alec.

When I had first found out about his feelings for her, I felt encouraged that he was showing interest in someone and that he was exploring those feelings. Alec guarded his emotions and rarely reached out to other people, so the fact that he had shared things with this girl seemed like a good sign regarding his emotional health. During one of our first visits to see Alec after his admission to Philhaven, he had asked us to tell the young lady that he loved her.

"This isn't something we can do for you," I had explained. "That's probably something you need to tell her yourself."

I thought back on this as the time drew near for me to share with him the news that she wasn't interested in anything more than friendship.

The therapist opened up that particular part of the conversation.

"Alec, your mother and father have something they want to talk to you about."

He turned a questioning gaze in our direction.

"We need to talk about your feelings toward your friend that you miss," I began. "There are things you need to know about her perspective on your friendship."

He looked back and forth from his mother to me. There was a glint of reluctance on his face, almost like he didn't want to hear anymore, as if he knew it was coming but if he didn't hear it, it wouldn't be true.

"Alec, she cares about you very much. She values you as a friend. But her parents have raised her to focus on being a teenager and not to enter a serious relationship while she's still in high school. She has no interest in being anything other than friends. It's nothing against you."

All along, I knew that the news would hurt him deeply. I only hoped that he would be able to deal with it better in that environment with a professional counselor to help him walk through the emotions. We finished talking and waited for his response.

It was not what I had hoped.

A shift occurred in his demeanor – he became more and more distressed with each passing moment. His eyes flashed from side to side as if he were trying to decide what to do. He looked desperate, crushed and in turmoil, and my heart broke for him. *First Kevin,* I thought, *and now this.*

The counselor, Diane, and I watched, trying to determine the next step in the discussion, but he began laughing quietly to himself and shaking his head. After a few seconds, he looked at me and waved his hand toward me.

"You need to get out of here," he said.

"Just me?"

"Both you and mom."

We sat in stunned silence, but the counselor spoke up.

"Perhaps the two of you should step out for a few moments and let me speak with Alec."

We agreed. I wasn't surprised that the conversation had gone this way, but I still had hope that we could work through it. I knew this represented yet another hurdle for Alec, so Diane and I waited patiently outside of the counseling room. I hoped the backwards step this brought about wouldn't undo all the progress he had made in the last week.

We talked briefly about his reaction, how hard that first rejection can be, and what those crushes can be like. I understood the pain he might be feeling, and his disappointment didn't surprise me. We speculated as to what else he might be feeling, but besides that, we sat quietly in some chairs just outside the office waiting to find out just how difficult it was going to be to get Alec over this new hurdle.

When the therapist opened the door, a grave expression covered her face.

"Could you come back in please?" she asked quietly.

I nodded, and we followed her back into the room. She moved slowly, tenderly, and her demeanor was drastically different. I immediately wondered what new, disturbing revelation Alec had shared. She sat down, and we took our seats. She leaned back, as if debating with herself on how to move forward.

"Alec has something to tell you," she said, her hands in her lap, looking not at Alec, but at us. Her expression was filled with compassion but also fear, as if she was already hurting for us. These changes that took place in her were unnerving.

What could Alec have possibly told her? I wondered.

Everything I have told you so far in this story has been my effort to provide you with an understanding and picture of the events, emotions, and history leading up to this very moment. What I was about to hear changed the course of my life forever and tested me in ways I didn't know possible, as a man and a father.

I looked at Alec, as if to encourage him to go ahead and say it.

He glanced at me, then at his mother, then back at me.

"I killed Kevin," he said.

10

He's Never Coming Home

I looked at Alec in silence.

I can't believe it. He did it.

That thought ran through my head over and over and over again, a million times a second. I wish I could say that his revelation took me off guard, but it did not. There had been times during the previous weeks where the thought had entered my head. It was obvious that whoever did this had known the family, had been in their house before. The attack had been so personal. Then, there were Alec's issues with anger, and, more recently, the dark thoughts he confessed to having.

Yet, each time the thought went through my head, I fought it. *No way, not Kevin. Alec wouldn't do that. He couldn't do it. I saw him the day it happened and again at the memorial service. No way.*

"Alec," Diane asked him, breaking the silence. "Did you really do this?"

Both of us wanted to believe that he was just making it up.

"I did it," he confirmed. "I killed Kevin and his parents."

I stared at him and tried to get a feel for where he was emotionally. I tried to determine whether or not he was being truthful. His mother began to cry softly. I glanced at her and saw only devastation. My mind raced into the future...what would this mean for Alec? For our family?

My God, I thought, *what did he do to that family? His best friend and his friend's parents? My son, my family, is responsible for their great pain and anguish.*

Then, the therapist spoke.

"Perhaps you are making this up, Alec," his counselor suggested. "Perhaps you are seeking attention or projecting this on to yourself after all the pain you have been through during the last few weeks. Isn't it possible that this trauma is confusing the truth inside of your mind?"

He paused for a moment.

"No, it's true," he said. "I'm not making it up."

He proceeded to share specific details that convinced us he had done it.

"You know how Mom works at night. I dressed in dark clothing, a dark coat, and I snuck out. I took a flashlight, and I wore gloves. I wore a black cap and taped over the logo. These are the shoes I wore that night," he said, motioning toward his feet.

His original plan was to go over and smother Kevin with a pillow or something. He didn't say who woke up first or when he took out the knife, but he did say that he killed Kevin along with his mother and father. Kevin's sister wasn't supposed to be home for a couple more days, so he didn't know she was in the house.

"I felt nothing but rage the whole time. Just rage, completely out of control. But afterwards I was scared. I ran from the house filled with this intense fear."

He paused for a moment.

"Are you sure you did this?" the therapist asked again. "There has been a lot of news coverage, and you've been through a lot. You could be taking this on as your own crime."

Alec's face was deadpan. He spoke as if he were telling us about a recent class he had taken or a movie he had seen.

"No, that's not true. I did it. Kevin died in the hallway facing the wall. His father lay on the bed with his head hanging over the side. His mother was just a few inches from the doorway. I ran behind their house – that's where I lost my cap and flashlight, 'cause I fell in the woods."

I was stunned. I kept waiting for him to say he was only kidding. That it was some kind of sick joke. But that never came.

"When I got back to Mom's house I cleaned up. She got back around five, and I was still awake. I told her I woke up earlier and couldn't get back to sleep."

When his mother heard him say this, and it lined up with the morning as she remembered it, it only served to upset her more. She wept harder. I went deeper into shock as I watched him retell this story in a calm demeanor, completely detached from what he was saying. There was relief in his words, too, as if he was glad to have finally told someone.

He never gave a motive that night, only said something about Kevin "annoying" him lately, and, ironically enough, we didn't ask "Why?" I think we were just too overwhelmed by everything that he was saying, and we wanted it to stop.

Then, silence filled the room. The four of us sat there staring at each other. None of us knew what to do or say, and finally, the therapist suggested that she contact someone. First, she got in touch with the psychiatrist on call that weekend, which happened to be the same doctor who had done Alec's initial evaluation. He advised her to go to the facility administrator. She made the call, and he told us to wait there until he came over.

More silence. More waiting. The therapist muttered a few things I can't recall – the situation was so extreme for everyone. She didn't know what to do or say, and I can't blame her. How can anyone be prepared to hear something like that? You can't. There is nothing you can be taught that would prepare you.

Meanwhile, in the silence, I stared at my 16-year-old boy, who just moments earlier had endless possibilities in the life ahead of him. But now his life was over, at least in the sense of all the hopes and dreams I had for him. He would never go off to college, never date, never marry. He would go to prison for the rest of his life. He would grow old there. He would die there.

What do you do with this kind of information? How would it affect the rest of the family? How would I protect the rest of my children?

My God, I can't believe he actually did this. Is this really happening? What will this do to him? Why did he do it? What could I have done to stop this? Should I have seen it coming? Where do I start and what do I do first?

I looked at Alec, and my heart ached for his lost future. Then, I thought of what he said he had done, and the horror of it washed over me. The poor Haines family. How could my family have been responsible for what happened to them? It was against everything I had ever taught him.

Eventually, the administrator arrived. It was most likely only a few minutes, but the wait was excruciating. I can't remember much of the conversation, but one phrase sticks in my mind to this day.

"We'll give you some time to do the right thing," he said.

Do the right thing.

It was obvious to me what he meant by this: we were expected to turn our son in, to tell the world that our son had brutally murdered his best friend and his best friend's parents.

Did he have any idea what he was asking me to do?

He left the room, and again, the four of us sat in silence. There seemed to be nothing else to say that hadn't already been said, nothing to think that hadn't been thought. Everything had begun to turn over on itself, running in an endless loop. We decided to call it an evening, and we all stood up. Alec and I looked at each other.

In his face, I recognized the little boy I loved so dearly. He looked at me as if to ask, *Now what should we do, Dad?* He wanted me to fix it, to make it better, but my own heart fell to pieces. I knew no answers. I couldn't make it go away; I didn't know what to do. Screaming in my mind were the words, *Alec, why did you do this? I can't fix this!*

Alec hugged his mother good-bye. She was in tears and seemed to feel the same loss, confusion, and pain that I experienced. She held the embrace for a long time. Then, I hugged him.

"I love you, Alec," I said. I had no idea what else to say. He was my boy, and I was supposed to take care of him, yet I didn't have a clue about what to do next.

In the recesses of my mind echoed the administrator's words.

"We'll give you some time to do the right thing."

I took a deep breath, gathered myself, and went to the car. I'm sure Alec's mother and I talked about Alec. Didn't we? What else would we have talked about? But the truth is, I can't remember a sentence of that conversation. We both felt overwhelmed with disbelief and shock. I felt numb, as if my mind and body were no longer connected. And I felt fear.

I was afraid, afraid for Alec, afraid for Drew, afraid for Amy, afraid for Lynn. Terrified. How would this affect my other kids? They would have to live the rest of their lives with what Alec had done. Would we have to move? Would the media destroy our family? How would people respond to us in public or at school functions?

What should I do?

A father's instinct is to protect his children, not turn them in, but how could I protect Alec in this situation? There wasn't just my son and family to consider – there was what I already knew to be the "right thing" to do. There was my responsibility to the community, and above all, my duty to the Haines family. My faith and sense of right and wrong told me what needed to be done. What had to be done.

But how could I turn in my own son?

This battle would be fought over and over in my mind, not easily won by either side. Deep down, I knew what the outcome would be. But sometimes the battles must be fought even when the result is a foregone conclusion. I went from anger to fear to pain to grief to denial and back to anger again. My mind raced, in complete turmoil. I didn't know what to do with this new place where I found myself.

Drew was spending the evening with one of his friends while his mother and I visited with Alec. Lynn planned on picking him up on the way to my house after she finished work. When I got home they weren't there, so I called Lynn.

"Hey, Lynn, where are you?" I asked.

"I'm just picking up Drew. What's wrong?"

She could detect the distress and strain in my voice. I guess it was pretty obvious. She asked if she should take Drew out for dinner, just to give me more time.

"Bring my son home," was all I could say, barely keeping my emotions in check. I just wanted him home. I wanted to know he was safe. I wanted him close.

When they got home, I wanted to spend one more "normal" night with Drew and Lynn, so, as we had discussed earlier that day, we got out a game. I didn't want to alarm him, and I clung to life as it could have been, perhaps as it should have been. The three of us played "Pay Day", and I did my best to act normal. But I was so distraught that I couldn't pay attention to the game. My mind wandered back to Alec, and Lynn sensed my distraction. She kept looking at me with questions in her eyes.

What is wrong?

She knew something big had happened. Later, she told me that she was 99.9% sure of what I was going to tell her.

But at the time I wondered, *How could I ever tell her? What would it do to our life together?* This was way more than anyone deserved to take on in a new marriage – this was supposed to be one of the happiest seasons of my life. Our wedding day was less than two months away, and we had so many plans to make. Then I felt guilty – how could I be thinking about a wedding at a time like this, with Alec facing jail for the rest of his life and the Haines family still mourning their loss?

Whenever my son played a card, I'd think about his future and Alec's future. Alec would never play another game with us in this room again. He would never be in this house again. Why?

Why?

A point came in the game when I looked at Lynn and she mouthed the words, "What is it?"

"He's never coming home," was my soundless reply. I wasn't sure if she understood what I had said. I couldn't believe I was actually saying it. Soon after that, we finished the game, and Drew, who had started off poorly, won. He was happy and smiling. I was glad he won. Seeing him smile was like a tiny ray of light on a very dark day.

Lynn and I put the game away, and Drew went into the basement to play a video game before bed. I staggered into the living room and collapsed on to the sofa. Lynn knelt in front of me on the floor.

"What is it?" she asked.

I blurted it out just as Alec had done a few hours earlier. How else do you communicate something such as that?

"Alec killed the Haines family."

Saying those words broke something in me, something that had stood for as long as it could possibly stand. Lynn took my hands into hers as I slumped forward. I crumbled. I cried like I have never cried before, and the tears turned into sobs. I couldn't control my emotions. The whole time I thought to myself, *I have to pull myself together. I can't let Drew see me like this. I need to protect him from this for as long as possible.*

Lynn and I moved outside to the back patio. We sat on the step. The light rain had stopped and the night turned into a typical summer evening: muggy and heavy and still. But nothing else was typical.

"What do I do?"

"The only person I can think to share this with is our pastor," she said. "I'll call him first thing in the morning."

Now, both of us were an emotional mess.

"We should take a walk," I suggested, still worried that Drew might overhear us.

As we walked out on to the street, I thought about how much had changed in such a short time. A few short hours ago, if I had taken a walk, somewhere in the back of my mind would have been the question: Are we safe? Where is the killer? Those questions, though, seemed like such distant concerns.

"I'm not even sure if I should call Alec tonight," I said. "I don't know what to say to him."

I had called him each and every night since he had been admitted into Philhaven. But on that night, I was disappointed, confused, violated – he had gone against everything I had taught him, everything I believed in.

"If he was sick with cancer, would you call him?" Lynn asked me. "This is no different. Tim, he's not well. He needs you now just as much as he would with any other sickness."

As her words sunk in, I knew she was right. He would need me more now than ever before. We weren't more than 100 yards from the house, but I decided to go back and call him.

I had no idea how it would go, and as I waited for the staff to retrieve Alec, I wondered what mood he was in, what his reaction would be to my voice on the phone.

I stood in the kitchen, and we spoke for fifteen minutes, during which I tried to comfort him. I let him know I would do whatever I could. But two things about that conversation still echo in my mind, both questions.

The first question was something I couldn't stop wondering:

"Alec, I need to know. Did you REALLY do this?"

"Yes, Dad, it's true."

The second was a question he asked me.

"Dad, what are you going to do?"

I paused. It was a vague question, but I knew exactly what he meant: was I going to turn him in?

"I don't know, Alec. I don't know what we are going to do."

I told him I loved him. I said goodnight. His question haunted my conscience and tested me in ways I couldn't have imagined.

What was I going to do?

11

A Pastor and a Lawyer

Wednesday morning finally arrived after a tormented, sleepless night. I was exhausted. Lynn and I had prayed for what felt like hours for Alec and our family. We knew we needed supernatural strength to face the challenges ahead.

But as questions began to mount, exhaustion threatened to drown me.

What would the next few days be like?

What would happen to Alec?

How could I protect my other children?

Certainly, we would have to move.

How would we deal with a relentless media?

And while all of these questions bounced around in my brain, one question rose up above all the rest:

How could I possibly turn in my son?

Then, I thought of the Haines family. They suffered such an immense loss – how could I do anything other than what was right by them? My family might be going through a tragedy, but their family had experienced even worse and at the hands of my son. I had to do what was right for them.

I knew at that point that I had to take things as they came. This meant, first of all, getting out of bed and going to work. I had brought work home the previous night but, for obvious reasons, hadn't gotten anything done. The stress and uncertain events in my future made it apparent that I would not be getting work done any time soon. I couldn't think straight. So I decided to go into the office, drop off the paperwork, and tell them I would be out for a few days.

I arrived just after 7am. I left notes for a few people not yet in, handed off some projects to co-workers, and looked for my supervisor. The CEO saw me and asked how things were going.

"Honestly, something so horrible has happened that you can't even imagine it. I can't talk about it now, but I need to be out for a little while."

"Do whatever you need to do, Tim. Take care of your family."

If you only knew, I thought to myself.

I looked rough, and just about every person I passed asked me what was wrong or if I was okay.

"I just can't talk about it today," I said, quickly passing by.

As I sat in my office making a few last notes for coworkers, a friend stopped by to see how I was doing. He knew that Alec was in Philhaven, and he could tell that I was having a difficult morning. He tried to pick me up by saying, "Some times things happen for a reason – the good thing is there is always a silver lining. Things can be fixed."

I looked up at him and said in a somber voice, "No, Greg, sometimes that's not the case. There's not always a silver lining, and sometimes you can't fix things."

He didn't know how to respond.

Finally, I got everyone up to date on the projects I was involved in and left. I found myself on the edge of losing it emotionally. I couldn't keep it together much longer. Besides, it was nearly 8:00 am, and I had a lot to do.

After a few phone calls to some friends, I got a reference for a criminal attorney. He came with the highest recommendation from another lawyer friend of mine – that was good enough for me. I'll call him David.

"Hi, I'm calling to set up an appointment," I told the receptionist.

"He's not going to be in until after 10:30 this morning – he's currently in court with another case. Can I take a message?"

"I really need to meet with him today. I know you probably hear this all the time, but this is an incredibly important and urgent matter."

I felt like I was in a movie. I imagined people calling her every day, their world falling apart. Why would she think I was any different?

"I understand, sir. I'll give him the message as soon as he comes in."

As I hung up, I thought to myself, *She probably hears that every day. I'll need to call her back.*

I called Lynn to tell her about the message I left with the attorney's office. She was working on scheduling a meeting with our pastor ASAP.

"Tim," she said, "I just can't get through to the church. I've been calling since 6am and I'm getting nothing but a busy signal. I'll call you back when I get through."

Eventually, Lynn called me back; she had been able to make an appointment for us at 11:30am – no small miracle, as it was a huge church and the pastor's schedule was usually full. It turns out that the church telephone lines had been down, but a friend of Lynn's was able to put Lynn in touch with our pastor's secretary.

What I did for the two hours between calling the attorney and leaving for the church, I can't recall. Huge gaps reside in my memory, and the moments I do remember are held together by incredible feelings of being overwhelmed, confused, in pain, lost, angry, desperate, and uncertain.

I tried to reach the attorney during my drive to the church. The same receptionist answered.

"David is back, and he has your message, but he is very busy."

I didn't want to talk about the situation over the phone, and certainly not with her, but at that point I realized that if I wanted to get a meeting with him, I'd have to let her know what it was regarding.

"I need to meet with David about the Haines case."

That was all it took.

"Please hold."

A few moments later her voice came back on the line.

"I'm going to transfer you to David's line. Please hold again."

She put me through to his office.

"Hello, Mr. Kreider?"

"Yes," I said. "Thanks for taking my call."

"My pleasure. I understand that you may have information pertaining to the Haines case?"

He sounded polite, but I could tell that he took my call mostly out of curiosity and was skeptical about any information I might disclose. I'm not being critical – there was so much speculation and anxiety in the community surrounding this event, and there were often things being reported or said that had no basis in truth. As far as David knew, I was just a concerned member of the community with some tidbit or rumor.

I tried to talk to him without giving away too many details, but that got us nowhere, and I could tell he was getting impatient. I finally just said it.

"My son has confessed to me that he committed the murders."

This immediately changed the tone of the conversation.

"Okay, Mr. Kreider, I'll rearrange my day. Could you meet me at my office at 1:30 this afternoon?"

I arrived at the church. Lynn was already there, waiting for me. She got out of the car, and the weight of the situation was written all over her face. I gave her a kiss and a long hug; then we held hands and walked into the pastor's office.

"Hi, Lynn. Tim. Good to see you two."

Suddenly, I realized he must think that we wanted to talk about our upcoming wedding. *If that were only the case,* I thought.

"Have a seat," he said kindly. "What can I do for you?"

I didn't know where to begin.

"Have you heard of the Haines family murders that took place over in Manheim Township a few weeks ago?"

Our church was in a different county, and our pastor has the same philosophy as I do when it comes to news: he doesn't follow events in the media very closely. As a result, he hadn't heard of the tragedy. I gave him a brief summary of the crime before saying that difficult sentence again, the one that I just couldn't wrap my brain around no matter how many times I said it.

"My oldest son has confessed to the murders."

His reaction would become the one I most typically received in the coming weeks, months and years. He sat there quietly, his eyes displaying the shock that he was trying to reign in. What does someone say when that information enters their mind? What do you do with it? How do you process it?

67

The three of us discussed it for a little while. He tried to provide us with comfort and some guidance. He offered us any support that he or the church could give.

"What can we do for you?" he asked.

We explained the course in front of us, or at least as much of it as we could see at that time. Then he prayed for us, for Alec and the rest of our family, as well as for the Haines family. He prayed that I would find the strength to do what I needed to do.

His support comforted me. It was soothing to be with him and Lynn, to know that I was not alone.

The words from his prayer echoed in my mind as I drove away from the church: "Give Tim the strength to do what he needs to do."

David's office was located on the second floor of a small commercial building. I drove along the front until I saw the sign for the law office, then pulled into one of the few spaces provided and shut off my car. Such moments of silence usually went one of two ways – intensely peaceful or incredibly overwhelming. I sat there quietly, reflecting on what I was about to do. Once I entered that office and told David what Alec had said, what I knew, there was no turning back.

Less than 24 hours before that moment, my greatest concern was how sick my son was and what I needed to do to help him get well and how long that might take. Now, those worries were eclipsed by the greater unknown; what would happen to Alec, and would he spend the rest of his life in prison?

Was there another way?

I sat there resting my hands on the steering wheel. I leaned forward, placing my head on to my hands. I gathered the strength I needed to get out of the car, wishing none of this had ever happened. Two voices shouted in my head: one said, "Hide! This isn't fair! Let someone else deal with it!" The other voice, a bit louder, shouted, "You know what you have to do – now get up and do it! Your son and your family need you!"

The interior of the building was aged, the walls covered by what appeared to be original wallpaper. As I walked up the stairs, the aroma from a neighboring Subway sandwich shop lingered in the air. On any normal day, that would have made me hungry, yet today it was offensive. I realized I hadn't eaten in 24 hours yet didn't feel a hint of hunger.

I gathered myself outside the door to the law office, then eased my way inside, knowing that each step took me closer to a point of no return. Just inside the door, a woman sat behind a desk in a modest waiting area.

"Hi, I'm Tim Kreider. I'm here to see David."

"Please take a seat," she said. "I'll let him know you're waiting."

I felt nervous, unsure of myself. I looked around the office, trying to get a feel for the kind of man to whom I would entrust my son's life. A picture of a baseball game from long ago hung on the wall. I loved playing baseball when I was a kid, and the picture (for a brief time) took me to another place, away from the pain and fear of the present day. It felt like a gift, a reminder that things had not always been this bad.

I looked closer. The batter's swing was frozen in time, and I wondered, did he hit the ball? Did he swing and miss? Was his team winning or losing? It looked like a beautiful summer day. Was the crowd cheering? I couldn't tell.

"Tim? Hi, I'm David."

I got up and shook his hand. It struck me that he looked tired, as if he carried a large burden. We walked through a small office where another woman worked, surrounded by stacked folders. I wondered about the lives represented by each folder and what circumstances had brought them into this office.

As we entered the room, he directed me over to a small table against the far wall covered in folders. David's office told me that he was down to earth, driven by results, not appearances. He worked hard and cared about what he did. Something about his face and his personality told me that I could trust him with my son.

"Can I get you anything to drink?" he asked me.

"No, thank you."

He asked questions about Alec. We reviewed the basic details leading up to Alec's confession. He made periodic notes on his yellow legal pad. When we finished talking, he paused, and I could tell that he was trying to decide whether or not to take the case.

"I'm currently handling another very high profile case," he said reluctantly. "It consumes most of my time. I just don't know if I can take on something else as big as this. But that case is coming to a close."

He paused. He looked tired, and I'm sure he knew that our case had the potential to be extremely long, difficult, and emotional. I could tell he was someone who cared about the people he represented. I tried to stay calm, but inside I began to feel anxious: what would I do if he decided not to take the case? Where would I go?

Then, he looked at me.

"I'll meet with Alec," he said. Relief flooded through me.

He called the front desk and rearranged his schedule for the rest of the day, then called his wife.

"I'll be home late tonight," he told her. I wondered how many times she got that call. For a moment, I was overwhelmed with gratitude for his dedication. It was obvious that he was a man who cared deeply about what he did and took the burden of it personally. Then he turned to me.

"I need to talk to Alec," he said.

12

A Mental Health Defense

I left my car at David's office, and he drove us to Philhaven, giving me the opportunity to fill him in on recent events.

"I know you don't know much about the case yet," I said, "but is there any chance that Alec could have a mental health defense?"

Again, I could see the same weight come over him that I had seen before. I knew this would be a difficult conversation.

"I need to tell you a few things that might be difficult to hear."

"Okay," I said, steeling myself.

"A mental health defense is very unlikely in Pennsylvania. The standard is high and very difficult to meet."

This disheartened me – based on what I saw and heard during the previous week, Alec was definitely sick and needed help. The possibility of a mental health defense had been my only hope.

"What are the possible punishments?" I asked hesitantly.

"Well, if there is any good news it's that, due to Alec's age, the death penalty is off the table."

The context of this conversation floored me. That was the good news? My son wouldn't be executed. That was the good news. After a few minutes of silence, during which I tried to come to terms with a situation in which this was "good news," I asked him another question.

"What will probably happen to Alec?"

He explained the difference between the varying degrees of murder convictions. He explained the significance of 1st, 2nd, and 3rd degree murder. I listened as he explained these things, knowing that I would need to communicate this information to Lynn and Diane later. But when someone is talking about life without parole for your sixteen year-old son with a best case of 20 years per count (60 years in Alec's case), it's hard to feel anything other than disbelief.

David shared with me that he had experienced great loss in his family involving one of his children. He didn't go into the details, but at that moment, I understood why he had decided to take on our case. He was a father. He could feel my pain. I could see the empathy in his face and now understood what I had sensed when we first met. He carried his own burden of loss.

I told him everything I could about Alec: his childhood, his personality, his interests, his anger, and his recent struggles. It's difficult to tell the story of someone's life in such a short time, but I tried to hit the more important moments, the things I thought he would be interested in hearing and that might be beneficial.

As our conversation continued, I sensed that he was being cautious regarding what he discussed with me, how much he told me, and what he said. I found this curious: I was Alec's father, right? Then he said something that explained all that.

"Based on what Alec told you and his mother, you will need separate counsel. I'll represent Alec, but you'll need to have your own attorney."

"Really? Why's that?"

Again, his answers seemed vague.

"Because of what you know, you could potentially be put at odds with Alec. I can't say anything else regarding that right now, except that you need to speak to someone else on your own."

"Could you recommend someone?"

He thought for a moment, then made a call and scheduled an appointment for us at 8:00am the next morning with an attorney I'll refer to as Brian. We rode the rest of the way to Philhaven in silence. My mind traced over the familiar, circular paths:

What should I do? What will this mean for Alec's future? How will this affect my family? What about the Haines family and their daughter? I can't believe my family is responsible for her loss! It's all so horrible. I can't believe I'm in this situation.

I glanced out the window and watched the countryside pass by me. This drive would never feel the same.

When we arrived at Philhaven, we checked in at the juvenile wing.

"The first thing I'd like to do is speak with a representative from Philhaven," he said as we walked down the hall. "In the meantime, Alec is not to discuss any further the conversation you had last night. Not with staff members, not with his mother, and not with you."

I nodded, and David walked into a different part of the hospital to speak with the administrators.

In the meantime, I found Alec's mother. I sat with her and explained who David was and what I had already learned from him. I told her how important it was that Alec not talk to us about what he had done or anything from the previous night. We tried to make small talk, but so much had changed in the previous 24 hours. Nothing else seemed important or worth discussing.

My son's future was hanging in the balance.

Eventually, David returned from speaking with the Philhaven staff. Then, he and Alec met in a small, private room. While they spoke, I tried to bring Alec's mother up to date on the sentencing information that David had shared with me on the ride up. She didn't take the news very well, especially about the death penalty not being a consideration – that only served to provide a heart-breaking picture of how desperate the situation had become.

"The most important item seems to be the 2nd degree murder charge," I explained to her, trying to remember what David had told me. "That carries a mandatory life sentence without any chance of parole and does not permit a mental health defense. If we can avoid this, there might be hope for Alec's future."

But it was far too early to know anything for certain.

I also told her about David's insistence that we obtain our own counsel. She was just as confused as I was about it – so much uncharted territory. We needed to trust the people around us for guidance.

David came out of the room and approached us.

"How did it go?" I asked him.

"It went fine." He paused for a moment. "I don't think that Philhaven is allowed to disclose Alec's confession to anyone, including the authorities."

He paused again.

"This means that, at this point, it is up to you and Alec's mother to decide what to do. If you don't say anything, there is no legal way the information can be shared."

I sighed, but not with relief. It would be up to us. There was no way out of this. He continued talking.

"Do not discuss any part of this with Alec. Do not discuss any part of your conversation with him from last night or any details about Alec's confession. I've reviewed this in detail with Alec. He knows not to talk about any of it with you."

David shook our hands and left. Alec's mother said she would give me a ride home, and we stayed around to spend some time with Alec. Philhaven provided us with the same small room so that we could have a private conversation.

Alec seemed more upbeat than he had been before his meeting with David.

"He told me that no one here at the hospital can tell anyone about my confession. As long as you guys keep quiet, no one will know."

I stared at him, trying to comprehend the significance of what was unfolding. My son didn't doubt that his mother and I wouldn't tell anyone. He believed everything would work out. I hadn't thought of this scenario until this moment. I would betray my son by going forward. How would he respond if I did that?

As long as you guys keep quiet, no one will know.

My reaction to Alec's words took on a different tone than Alec expected. Alec detected my uncertainty. He kept looking at me. He knew of my faith, my belief in doing the right thing, my convictions surrounding things like responsibility and accountability. He and I had spoken many times over the years about these specific issues, and he knew that I held myself and my children responsible for their actions. Concern crept on to his face. He didn't know what I would do.

"The knife's still in the house," he said, at first in passing, but then his voice took on a concerned tone. "What if someone finds it?"

You are not supposed to be talking about this stuff, I thought to myself. *For being so smart, how could you be so dumb?*

"What will you do if you find it?" he asked, implying that we should get rid of it.

"We shouldn't be talking about this," I said, interrupting him. "Your mother and I don't need to know anything more about this."

When the time came to leave, I hugged him almost desperately, not wanting to let go of him. Just thinking about the things that might happen in the coming days overwhelmed me.

During the drive home, his mother and I discussed what we were going to do. We went back and forth – we could be quiet about what Alec told us. A parent's instinct is to protect their child at all costs. Our conversation then turned to the knife. What should we do if we found it? Should we turn it over to the police? What was the right thing to do?

The internal conflict intensified. Alec was our son. We should protect him. We might "lose" him for the rest of our lives. What kind of life would he have behind bars? We were desperate for a way out, but I just didn't see one – after all, this didn't involve just our family. Alec killed three people in a horrific fashion. They lost three family members. A young lady would never see her parents or brother again.

And my son had done it – the same son for whom I had such hopes and dreams, a son I loved. But he was the same person who had taken all of these things away from another family. They deserved justice and resolution.

Could we let our son get away with murder?

13

The Long, Dark Night

Alec's mother dropped me off at my car, and we agreed to go to the attorney's office together the following morning. We would make up our minds regarding turning Alec in after that meeting. Barely 24 hours had passed from the time he had confessed to us. Exhaustion overwhelmed me. My arms and legs felt heavy. My heart was even heavier.

How was I going to do this?

I called Alec and spoke with him briefly. There didn't seem much to say after all that had happened.

"Look, Alec, I love you. I will be with you through whatever comes."

A moment of silence.

"Dad," he asked hesitantly. "What are you going to do?"

"I don't know yet. I don't know."

It was obvious that he expected me to keep quiet, to protect him. Was that such an unreasonable expectation for a son to have of his father, that I would protect him?

For the first time, a new and disturbing thought entered my mind: What would happen to my relationship with Alec if I went to the authorities? He'd never understand! He'd feel as if I had betrayed him! If I loved him, how could I do this? How could I hand him over to the police?

That's what he would think, anyway. He'd hate me. I'd lose him twice: first, to prison, where the future I wanted for him would vanish. Then, I'd lose my relationship with him – he'd hate me for what I did. Who could blame him? He would be in prison because of me, because of his father.

A mental whirlwind raged through my mind, shaking the conviction I felt earlier in the car. Perhaps I should protect my son? Maybe there was a way out?

Where was the knife? I thought about looking for it. If I found it, I could get on my motorcycle, ride out to the bridge that crosses over the Susquehanna River and toss it into the water below. It was the middle of the night – I could take back, country roads, winding my way across the county so that no one would see me. I'd know if someone was following me.

I could do it.

No one would ever know.

His mother and I could go through our homes and take everything out that might link Alec to the murders: clothes, hats, anything and everything that may have been involved. Philhaven wasn't permitted to tell anyone. If we destroyed the evidence, how would they ever link the crime to Alec? Was it possible?

Alec still had a chance, but it was up to me, and we were running out of time. If I was going to do this, it had to be tonight. My pulse quickened, adrenaline pumped through my body. I couldn't sleep. There hadn't been anything in the media about evidence found, and Alec thought that all he lost was a flashlight and a hat. If we were lucky, there wouldn't be anything else that led to Alec.

But I couldn't do nothing.

It isn't right! I thought to myself. *I know it isn't right. I've spent a lifetime telling my children to do the right thing, no matter what, and to be accountable. No matter the circumstances. It is always about their choices. Don't look for the easy way out. Do what is right.*

This seemed different though. This involved my son's future, my son's life. His entire life! This seemed so big that maybe all of those platitudes didn't apply. I tried everything to convince myself not to go to the authorities – no one would blame me if I tried to make it go away. They would understand. Many other people would do the same thing, doing whatever it took to protect their child.

For a moment, protecting Alec became the tough path, the path that took strength and fortitude. *The tough thing is to be quiet and try to hide this,* I tried to convince myself. *The easy thing would be to go to the authorities.*

My mind lost its perspective for a few moments in the middle of that very dark night. I wanted so desperately to spare my family from the approaching pain that I became willing to consider any option. The ideas got more and more outlandish as my mind wandered along that path of denial and sadness.

I can break Alec out of Philhaven. There isn't much security. They never search me when I visit. I went there for over a week; people recognize me and I always cooperated. They would never expect it. Alec's relationship with the staff was good, and they allowed him to walk me to the door when I left. The hospital placed him on suicide watch, 24/7, but there was never more than one guy with him, and he was never very big. Alec and I could definitely get out the door – after that, it was a short trip through the hall and down the stairs. Then, freedom.

Wait a minute! What am I thinking!

I remembered my other children, my engagement to Lynn. Where could Alec and I go? We'd be on the run forever. What a ridiculous thought! There wasn't just my own family to think about – the Haines family deserved justice. If I had lost both of my parents and my brother, I would want (and deserve) to know what had happened and gain some sort of closure, at least regarding the crime. That poor girl didn't have her family with her any longer – no one to share her joys or sorrows. They wouldn't be at her graduation from college, her marriage. Her holidays would feel empty for a very, very long time, maybe for the rest of her life.

My son still lived. Exchanging one life for the three taken is what it came down to. I would still be able to write to him, talk to him, and see him. The Haines family lost that because of what Alec had done. They never had a chance to say good-bye.

And the terror they must have felt on that final night? Just thinking about the pain, the fear, and the horror of their final moments on earth haunted me. I felt sick to my stomach. I realized I had no right to feel sorry for myself. Thinking of the Haines family took me back to their memorial service, their grief, and the song the man sang.

Seeing that sun, in the middle of that night, or even imagining its existence, seemed impossible. Nothing was alright. Nothing would ever

78

be alright. Not for the Haines family, not for my family. The situation was winless, hopeless.

The internal struggle continued throughout the night. I don't remember sleeping. But that battle was an exercise in futility because one thing was for certain: deep inside, at the core of who I was, I knew what I had to do.

I just didn't know how I was going to do it.

14

The Bridge-Keeper's Son

Thursday morning arrived, and the weight of my burden increased to nearly unbearable levels. The first, exhausting week of Alec's stay in Philhaven held nothing compared to these past 36 hours. Less than two days had passed since Alec's confession. I'd barely slept or eaten. I hadn't shaved. Nothing seemed important; nothing mattered except for the task at hand. I needed all of my energy to simply keep moving and do what had to be done. I got dressed in shorts and a t-shirt and waited for Alec's mother to arrive.

We didn't talk much during the 15-minute drive to the attorney's office in downtown Lancaster. A feeling of inevitable doom hovered in the car. I held on to the thinnest thread of hope that this new attorney, able to speak more openly than David, would give us more encouraging information.

Maybe, just maybe, there was a way out? I wanted to think so. I searched for hope. I wanted to avoid the path that stared me in the face.

You can't get out of this, I thought to myself. *There isn't a way out, and you know it. Accept it and do the right thing. There is no other choice.*

We pulled into a parking space around the corner from his office a few minutes before 8:00am. The building, an old Victorian home, sat on the corner. Several desks filled the first room we walked into – the high ceilings and decorative wood trim provided a complete contrast to

David's office. Brian kept his spacious office orderly and expertly decorated with a masculine theme. We sat in chairs facing his desk.

"So?" he asked. "What can I do for you? I've only been told that the matter is urgent, and that it's important we meet."

"We're here to talk about the Haines' case," I said.

"I wondered if that was it," he said. "I couldn't think of anything else going on in the community that would have required such urgency."

I nodded.

"My son has confessed to the murders," I said.

He took it in stride and showed no significant reaction or emotion, going straight to the task at hand. He asked questions surrounding the events and what we knew. We gave him a brief overview of the previous eight days, starting with the events at Diane's house the Tuesday before.

"What are our options?" I asked him.

"You have two options," he said matter-of-factly with very little emotion in his voice. "You can keep quiet and hope no one ever finds out, or you can go to the authorities with what you know. The events of the past week will probably bring attention to Alec, if they haven't already: he was one of Kevin's friends, and now he's been admitted to Philhaven for threatening suicide. It may only be a matter of time before they look closer at Alec. But if you keep quiet, you never know what will happen."

There was no magic option, no new way forward that would make it good for everyone, free Alec, and bring back the Haines family. I knew in my head that there wasn't, but that meeting had been my last hope. The most poignant moment came next.

"You do know, if you go to the authorities with this, you've lost your son?"

That statement hit me like a sledge hammer.

"In Pennsylvania, the death penalty is not a consideration for Alec because of his age," Brian continued. "But he still will most likely spend the rest of his life in prison without the chance of parole. You will be able to visit him, write to him, and talk to him on the phone from time to time, but his future will be gone. The media will pursue your family relentlessly. Your life is about to be turned upside down."

I had thought through all of this before, but hearing it from someone else, out loud, for the first time, proved difficult.

He explained to us the varying degrees of murder convictions, reviewing what David had already told me. The biggest deal was that first and third degree murders allowed for a mental health defense.

"But this is very difficult to prove in Pennsylvania and unlikely to succeed," he said. Everywhere I turned, everyone was telling me the same thing: even though Alec was extremely sick, he had little chance in obtaining a mental health defense.

I shared with him some of the issues that came out of Alec's treatment at Philhaven as well as his past history. I wanted to believe that Alec had a chance.

"It's a long shot, at best," he said with a slight shake of his head, regret in his voice.

But you weren't there, I thought to myself. *You don't understand how sick he really is.*

We thanked him for his time, told him we'd have to think about what to do, and said we'd let him know later in the day. I knew what I was going to do, but I also knew that Diane had not yet accepted what we needed to do. It was important to me that we both agreed on the next step.

We walked back out to the car. We climbed in and sat there, not moving, not saying anything. Finally, Diane asked the question.

"How can we turn in our son?"

This was the question. The question was never, "What's the right thing to do?" or "How can we keep Alec out of prison?" For me, the question always assumed that we knew the right thing. The question was always "How?"

"We have to. It's our only option."

"I know, but..."

More silence. We just sat there. How can I explain the unspoken feelings and emotions that travel through the silence between parents considering such a difficult decision? But as I sat there, a story came to mind, one that I had heard a few months before at church. I shared it with her.

During the depression era, there was a man fortunate enough to have a job when many people in the country went without the basics in life. He gave thanks every day for this job and took his responsibility seriously.

82

He worked for the railroad and oversaw a bridge that stretched over the river. The man often raised the bridge for the many ships crossing beneath it, but he always had to lower it again when the passenger train arrived.

The man worked at the bridge for many years, and while he and his wife continued to be thankful for all that the job provided him, they could not have children. Years passed, many trains traveled over the bridge, many boats went under it, and yet the couple could not have children. Then the day came that he and his wife had so longed for. She was pregnant.

Eventually, they received the gift of a beautiful son. This child meant the world to him, and as the boy grew, so too did the father's love for him. As the boy grew older, the father began to look forward to all the wonders he would experience and all of the things they would share. One day, the boy came to him with a question:

"Can I go to the bridge with you?"

An overwhelming sense of pride and happiness filled the bridge keeper.

"Of course!" he said.

The next day, they packed a lunch and headed off to work together, father and son. When they got there, he showed his son the tower where he worked and explained what he did. Several large ships approached, coming up the river, and the father raised the bridge so that the ships could pass. Then the father had an idea: they should go down and sit on the bank together and eat their lunch where they could watch the ships pass.

His boy was amazed by the ships and proud that his father was the one that let them pass. The bridge keeper and his son were having such a wonderful time that the father lost track of the time. Suddenly, this beautiful father and son moment was interrupted by a sound that sent panic into the father's heart.

It was the whistle of the 1:00 passenger train.

The bridge keeper looked at his watch and realized he only had a few minutes to get to the control booth and lower the bridge. If he didn't, the passenger train would tumble into the river! The lives of hundreds of people on the train depended on him getting the bridge down in time. He turned to his son.

"Don't move. I have something very important to do. I'll be right back. Stay here. I promise. I'll be right back." He shouted these words over his shoulder while running up the bank.

The control booth was at the top of the tower on the river bank. He sprinted up the bank. His heart pounded. He was already panting when he reached the base of the tower, but he still had many ladders to climb in order to get to the control tower. The whistle to the train blew again. It was getting much closer. Little time remained. He began climbing as fast as he could. His heart was racing. He had to hurry. Again, he heard the whistle blow, and the train was so much closer. So little time!

Finally, he climbed into the control booth. Off in the distance, he saw the train speeding toward the bridge. His body shook after the long climb, and he tried to catch his breath. Sweat dripped down his forehead. But everything was all right. He had made it in time. The only thing left to do was pull the control lever and the bridge would lower for the train. He wiped the sweat from his face and put his hand on the lever.

Then, he heard something more terrifying than the whistle of the train: a voice cried out from far below him.

"Father, help me!" What was that? Again, he heard the cry.

"Father, help me!"

He ran to the window and looked down. To his horror, he saw his young son trapped in the gears of the bridge. The boy hadn't listened, hadn't stayed safely on the bank and watched the boats. He had tried to follow his father. He had tried to climb the ladders but had fallen in amongst the gears.

His father looked down at him. It was within his power to save his son, but he couldn't climb down the tower to his son and still get back up to the control booth in time to lower the bridge for the passenger train. If he lowered the bridge, his son would be killed.

What could he do? His mind raced. *The life of my son or the lives of people I don't even know.*

His son cried out again.

"Father, help me!"

The train grew closer and closer with every passing second. What was the right thing to do? His son meant everything to him. But he was responsible for the lives of everyone on that train. He looked at the train, and the bridge and thought of his son. He only had seconds to make a decision. He placed his hand on the lever to the bridge. Sweat was running down his face again; it was burning his eyes. His heart felt like it was in this throat. He felt weak and sick at the thought of what he must do. There must be another way!

The time was now! He had to make a decision. He closed his eyes and pulled the lever.

The bridge lowered just in time for the train to streak across the bridge. He watched the train speed by in front of him. He saw people sipping their drinks. Some were reading books and newspapers. Others were talking and laughing. They were clueless to the heart-wrenching sacrifice someone had just made. Their lives were not affected. To them, it was as if nothing had happened. As if no life and death choice had just been made. He watched them go by as tears ran down his face and sorrow filled his heart.

"Do you know!" he screamed as the train passed. "Do you know what I did for you! Do you have any idea!"

Then, the train was gone.

Diane and I cried in the car as I finished telling the story. We couldn't contain the pain and sorrow.

"I know we have to do it," she said. "I just wish there was another way."

We rode back to my house in silence.

15

The Missing Knife

As soon as I was in the house, I called our attorney, Brian, and told him to contact the police. I was going to come forward with everything that I knew. I would set the process into motion. I had no idea what to expect or how fast things would move. My only experience with this sort of thing was what I had seen on television and read in the newspaper. I wondered how much of it was real. What was going to happen to us?

Lynn and my youngest son had planted a garden, and Lynn was out back weeding. I sat alone in the house, waiting to hear from our attorney on what the next steps would be in regards to reporting what Alec had told us. What next?

The knife. Where was the knife?

The thought shot to the front of my mind. Was it in my home? I needed to know. For some reason it, became an all-encompassing thought, one I couldn't let go of. I had to find it.

I started by searching Alec's desk in the kids' room. He had left his large black bag sitting there on the floor. I took a deep breath and opened it, but there was nothing inside. I checked all the drawers in the desk. Nothing. I walked upstairs to his bedroom and looked in his closet.

Three Japanese swords lay on the floor inside his closet – he enjoyed looking at them. Could he have used one? Two of the three were too large, but maybe the smaller one? I pulled it out of its sheath and looked closer. It was almost a foot long and the blade was wide, not very sharp. I stared at it for a long time, but it didn't make sense. I looked through his karate bag, also on the floor. Nothing.

Only one other place remained for me to look – in the dark wood dresser. It had a couple of pull drawers on the bottom and two doors on the top, where he stored books, souvenirs, and clothing. I opened the left door and looked inside. A couple books, some miscellaneous items, and a small journal were stacked inside. I picked up the journal.

Then, I saw it.

I reached into the dresser and pulled out the black sheath. The knife still rested inside. When Alec was 12 years old, he had asked if he could have it. I grew up hunting and fishing a lot, and that was the knife I had always used. I had also received it when I was 12, so when he asked for it, I felt like I was handing a part of my childhood down to him.

I held it in my hand for a long time, just staring at it. The smooth black handle. The silver knob on the end, and the 4 to 5 inch blade still inside the sheath. I remembered giving it to him, warning him that if he did anything inappropriate with it, he would lose it.

Would he really have used this knife?

All of these thoughts swirled through my mind as I pulled the knife from the sheath in a slow, smooth action. As soon as I saw the blade, my heart sank – not that it was covered in blood. In fact, it was perfectly clean. But the tip of the blade was broken off. I could only imagine how or what had caused that – I gave him the knife in perfect condition. I knew in my heart that this was the knife. I just knew it.

Then, Lynn came into the room.

"Hey," she said, "what are you doing?"

I turned to her, holding the knife.

"This is the knife. It was a gift I gave to him. It was mine when I was a kid."

Her face filled with pain for me, a look I had seen too many times during the previous eight days.

"What are you going to do with it?"

She knew my thoughts from the previous night. I hesitated, still wanting to "help" my son.

Get rid of the knife! a voice shouted in my head. *This is your last chance! Get rid of it!*

But I knew I wouldn't get rid of it. I had already made that decision.

Finding the knife created a new dynamic in the situation. Now, we not only had my testimony of Alec's confession – we also had the murder weapon, a key component in proving any murder case.

Our attorney called later that day with an update.

"There are a lot of rumblings," he said. "Rumors. I'm in discussions with the D.A.'s office. The first conversation hasn't yielded an agreement on how to proceed, but we're getting there."

He was all over the situation, and I could tell he was completely comfortable with everything that was going on.

"I have the knife."

"You have the knife?" he asked. He was closely tied in with the legal community and had heard details about the crime that other people hadn't. "What kind of knife?"

"It's small. The blade is around four or five inches long."

"A smooth blade?" he asked.

"Yeah."

We both stopped talking as the serious nature of what we were talking about sank in.

"That sounds like the murder weapon. I know it was a small knife with a smooth blade. Well, this gives me more to go to the D.A. with. I'll speak with David, and we'll go from there."

"What are you aiming for?" I asked.

"The best thing that could happen at this point would be for them to take 2nd degree murder off the table – that's the only charge that won't permit a mental health defense. Since guilt will not be in question, that's the only path that might give Alec any chance of having a life outside of prison."

"You know that I'll cooperate," I said. "I just want my son to have a chance. That's all."

"I know, Tim. Look, taking murder two off the table isn't a big risk for the D.A. If Alec isn't deemed to have diminished mental capacity or to be insane as legislated by the State, he'll be convicted of 1st degree murder."

"Thanks for your help with this," I said. "I know he doesn't have much, but I'd at least like him to have a chance."

I called Diane, and we talked about when to tell Amy and Drew about Alec. They could tell something was wrong, but we hadn't told them much, only that Alec was very sick and we were trying to help him. We realized that things were going to start happening quickly, and we wanted to control when and where they found out, so we made the decision to tell them.

Diane brought Amy over to the house. My daughter had just turned 19; Drew was only 13. How do you break this kind of news to your own children? They had both known Kevin and spent time with him when he came to our house. My daughter had been visibly shaken by his death – she couldn't understand why anyone would do that to their family. Now I had to tell her that it was Alec. He had done it. Her own brother!

Drew and I waited for them in the kitchen. Since the divorce, we hadn't gotten together as a family very often – those times were few and far between and always involved something important. I think they probably knew that this meeting would be something about Alec.

Amy and Diane came into the kitchen. I don't remember the words I used to communicate that terrible news. All I know is that somehow I told them that Alec had confessed to the murders. Drew stood there quietly, his eyes welling up. Amy burst into tears immediately – I tried to hug her, but she pulled away and collapsed to her knees on the kitchen floor.

Diane knelt down beside her, and I sat down beside them and hugged Amy. Then, Drew came over and the four of us held each other, huddled there on the kitchen floor.

Diane, Amy, and I were all crying. Drew was stoic and showed only a little emotion.

"Why?" my daughter asked.

"Alec is very sick. He needs help," I said. Other than that, I didn't have any answers for her.

After the storm cloud of emotion passed, we all sort of leaned back.

"It's important that you guys not talk to anyone else about this," I explained. "We are trying to take care of things today, but for now, you need to stay quiet. We're doing everything we can to help Alec."

At this point, I didn't tell them that I planned on speaking to the police. Drew went home with Diane – I wanted to spare him any conversations I would have later that day with the attorneys or the police. As they walked out the door, I wondered, *Was this the right time to tell them? Should I have waited? Would there ever have been a right time?*

Just after noon of the same day, our attorney called.

"The D.A. has gone to the family," he explained. "They are willing to take 2nd degree murder off the table in exchange for your cooperation. The authorities want to get the knife and have you give your statement as soon as possible, some time today. Alec's attorney is aware of what you are doing, and he has agreed with me that this is a reasonable path for you to take."

This encouraged me. Perhaps if Alec's attorney could see the wisdom in my decision to go to the police, there was hope that Alec would understand. At that point, I couldn't imagine coping with Alec's hatred of me on top of everything else. I knew that soon enough I would need to face Alec and explain why I did what I was about to do.

The wheels of justice began to move. I could no longer stop them. From here on out, any control I attempted to maintain over Alec's future would be an illusion. The gears were turning. They were bigger than any of us.

Alec's sister and younger brother had not seen or spoken with him since his admission into Philhaven – it was so important to me that they see him before everything changed, before the process began. I got in touch with Philhaven, and we received approval for a family visit that evening, during which more than two people would be permitted to visit at one time.

So I would get one more opportunity to spend time with all three of my children, together. I had no idea when, if ever, we would have this opportunity again. Perhaps we could play a game and find some laughter and joy in each other's company. Perhaps we could talk about funny memories and times we had together. One last family moment.

At least I would have that.

16

The Flashlight

The afternoon dragged on. I became anxious. When were the police going to come over? When would I be questioned?

Finally, Brian called.

"They want to come over and pick up the knife."

"When is everything going to happen?" I asked him.

"I'm not sure, but it's going to be today."

I hung up the phone and for a moment felt panic rising up inside of me. Visiting time started around 4:30 and went until about 8:00. I needed to spend that time with my family. I wanted to be there with all my children.

I brought the knife down from Alec's room, took it out of the sheath, and placed both the knife and the sheath separately on a towel on the kitchen counter. Flashbacks went through my mind of times when I used that knife as a child: cutting my fishing line or sharpening a stick. I never could have imagined what my own son would eventually use it for.

Lynn came home early from work to provide some much needed moral support.

"I'm worried I'm going to miss our scheduled visit with Alec," I said.

"It's important to you," she said. "You should just go. I'll stay here and let the police in. I can show them the knife."

I thought about it for a moment.

"Thanks, but I don't think I should. This is too important – they want to take care of everything today, and I don't want to jeopardize the small chance Alec might have. If I don't cooperate, then what?"

My attorney finally called again.

"The police are on their way – they should be there soon. I'm coming over, too. I want to make sure it's all done properly."

I think he knew that I needed the moral support. The situation weighed on me more and more as the day passed. It seemed less and less likely that this was actually happening to my family – was I dreaming? Hallucinating? How could this be possible?

Around 4:00pm, three officers arrived at the house, accompanied by Brian. None were in uniform. Two of them were state police: younger, clean-cut guys in dark suits. The other one, from the township, looked to be about my age and wore a sports jacket and slacks. I recognized him when he came in, but I couldn't place him.

"Come on in," I said, leading them to the kitchen and showing them the knife.

Then, the township officer recognized me.

"Did you ever coach soccer?"

I told him I had, a few years before.

"That's why I recognize you. You coached my son's team."

My youngest son had played on the team with his boy. He asked about Drew.

"And how are you holding up?" he asked, genuine concern in his voice. He was a father, and he had a son that he loved. At least on that level, he could relate to the torment and pain that I felt. I sensed an unspoken compassion from one father to another. The look on his face seemed to communicate to me, *I don't know what I would do if I was in your place, but man, my heart goes out to you.*

He took some photographs of the knife.

"Do you mind if I wrap the knife in the towel and take it with me?"

"That's fine with me," I said. "I just want this over as quickly as possible."

"Where did you find the knife?" one of the state troopers asked me.

"In a dresser in Alec's room."

"Can you show us where that is?"

Just before we went upstairs, one of the officers saw pictures on my refrigerator.

"Are those of your son?"

I pointed to one of the photos.

"That's a picture of Alec and his sister at her graduation."

Alec was hugging his sister and had a huge smile on his face. He was so happy. My daughter, too, was ecstatic. Her joy in the moment was contagious. A thought flashed through my mind: I would never see Alec graduate from high school. I would never share the same moment with him.

Another photo of Alec hung on the refrigerator. In it he was much younger, wearing eyeglasses, and holding up a miniature golf club, smiling for the camera. He looked so little. I pointed to that picture.

"And that is him a long time ago."

I barely got the words out and had to choke back a sob. I cleared my throat.

What will happen to my boy? Look! He was happy once. What he did, that's not really him! Look! He is just a boy!

I walked out of the kitchen quickly. Tears welled up in my eyes, and I thought I was going to lose my composure. The officers sensed my difficulty and followed me upstairs without any further questions. I was impressed with their kind demeanor and sensitivity. We walked down the hallway to Alec's room.

I opened the dresser door and showed them where I found the knife, then moved out of the way, leaning against the doorway of Alec's room. Brian had stayed downstairs with Lynn, so I watched as the police officers took photos of the area where I found the knife.

"We need to do a quick visual search of the room," they explained. But there wasn't much light in Alec's room, and the dresser was deep, so it was difficult to see inside. I heard one of the officers ask the other a question.

"Do you have a flashlight?" he whispered to his partner.

I noticed how they were dressed and thought, *There's no way either of those guys brought a flashlight.* Then, it occurred to me that they were going to probably ask me for a flashlight.

I can't believe this! They're going to ask me for a flashlight! I just know it! They don't have one, and they're going to ask me! These thoughts ran through my head, and if the situation hadn't been so tragic, this internal dialogue would have been humorous to me. As it was, I had a wry little smile on my face just waiting for them to ask me.

They spoke quietly to each other, but I didn't listen because I knew what was about to happen. Then, one of the officers turned to me sheepishly.

"Mr. Kreider, do you have a flashlight?"

I could tell he was embarrassed. I let out a small exhale, a quiet laugh, thinking to myself, *You've got to be kidding me. I'm handing you my son and the murder weapon in a case where you had nothing, and now you want me to help you gather more information?* I wasn't angry. It was just another ridiculous moment in a surreal situation.

"Sure, I probably have one," I told them, exiting the room and walking downstairs. My attorney was coming up.

"What's going on?"

"They need a flashlight."

He gave me a look of disbelief, then walked back to the bedroom. I grabbed a flashlight in the kitchen.

"They need a flashlight," I said to Lynn, who greeted me with the same look of disbelief. "Maybe I should help them search, too."

I handed the flashlight to my attorney who was waiting at the top of the stairs.

"Isn't this going above and beyond the call of duty?" I asked him.

He looked at me as if to say, *I know, just hang in there.*

I went back downstairs, needing to get away from the situation. I was glad my attorney was up there – he would keep an eye on things. He knew how these things should go. His confidence and "take control" attitude comforted me. I stayed in the kitchen with Lynn, unable to relax, pacing back and forth. I looked at the pictures of Alec again, and my heart broke. If I stopped moving, I might never start up again.

After a short time, everyone came back downstairs. The search was over. I could tell that everyone struggled along with me – no one wanted to make this more difficult than necessary. I appreciated their compassion and understanding.

"I want to talk to you alone for a minute," my attorney said. We started to leave the kitchen, but I paused, looking back over my shoulder at the officers. My flashlight sat on the counter in front of them. They caught my eye as I looked over my shoulder.

"Just wanted to make sure you guys aren't stealing my flashlight," I said.

They smiled, and that small comment relieved some of the tension.

Brian and I stood in the next room.

"They want a testimony from you soon – probably tonight."

"Okay," I said. "I understand."

But inside, I was crushed. It was beginning to look like I wasn't going to make it to Philhaven for time with my children. That felt like the final blow – I had provided the authorities with the weapon, was willing to give my testimony, and had pretty much supplied everything they needed in the case against my son. I felt an immense amount of guilt. Now I wouldn't make it to what might be our last time together as a family.

Why wouldn't I be there? Because I would be at the police station, betraying my son.

Be strong, I told myself. *Protect the rest of the family. Cope.*

But I didn't feel strong; I didn't know if I could cope.

I felt broken.

17
The Testimony

My attorney walked out with the officers. I was to follow them to the municipal building in the next 20 minutes or so. I tried to gather myself, but the experience had shaken me. Sleep had eluded me for days. I didn't want to eat. My strength was beginning to fade.

"I have to give my statement tonight," I told Lynn. "I'm not going to make it to Philhaven."

"What?" she exclaimed, obviously angry. "I don't understand! Why can't they do it tomorrow? It's so unfair. I'll go there for you and explain why you can't come tonight – they are open 24 hours! You should be with your family!"

I nodded, but I didn't have the strength to change the course I was on. I didn't want anything to look out of place – Alec's future might depend on my cooperation. My body and mind felt numb. Everything felt beyond my control.

I called Diane, already on her way to Philhaven.

"I can't make it tonight. The police want me to give my statement." I tried to explain everything to her, but the emotions were too much. I almost broke down. "Promise me you'll tell Alec that I love him and that I want to be there more than anything."

"I'll tell him you can't make it because you're doing everything you can to help him," she said.

"Thank you," I said. I wanted to tell him in person what I was doing and why. Besides, I wanted him to enjoy his last visit with his brother and sister. At least they could have that time together, even if I couldn't.

Finally, I couldn't bear being at the house any longer. I had to go to the station, and Lynn insisted on going with me. We got in the car, and she held my hand as I drove. I was so thankful she was there – she had been a rock of support and faith through all of this. Moments came during those days when I worried about how the whole experience would impact our relationship. We went from a couple planning their wedding to a couple struggling through one of the most difficult situations anyone can imagine.

What disrupted my world disrupted hers. My pain and grief were hers. I didn't want her drawn into the media frenzy. She was involved in politics and owned her own business – how would this affect the rest of her life, her goals and dreams? It didn't seem fair to her. Our wedding was scheduled for August 5th, less than two months in the future! There was so much for us to do, to plan, but I couldn't bring myself to even think about it. I couldn't focus on anything but each moment, each day.

We arrived at the police station – it's about a half mile away and took literally a minute to get there – and walked into the lobby. After I told the attendant behind the glass who I was, he gave Lynn and I nametags and asked us to have a seat.

"Someone will be with you soon," he said.

That's strange, I thought. *I assumed they would want me back there immediately. What did they have going that was more important than this?*

Lynn went outside to call her family and let them know what was going on – it was the first time they had heard about Alec and all that had happened. She was outside for about ten minutes, and I waited for her, quietly looking around the lobby, wondering what her family would think. Lynn and I weren't even married yet. I wouldn't blame them if they told her to get as far away from this situation, and me, as possible. Why would anyone want to take on all that this meant, and how it was likely going to change our lives? Lynn and her family didn't deserve any of this.

She came back in, and we didn't say much, just kept waiting. We both looked at the bulletin board in front of us, covered with various notices and announcements, but one stood out to me as being more prominent than the others:

A $25,000 reward to anyone providing details regarding the Haines' Case leading to an arrest and conviction.

I pulled the notice off of the bulletin board and let it fall to the floor. As far as I was concerned, there was no longer a need for it, and no one would be collecting it.

"What was that?" Lynn asked me quietly.

"It's a reward notice," I said in a monotone voice.

She looked at me with compassion, then stood up, walked over to where it lay on the floor, picked it up, and placed it in the trash can under the table. Then, she sat down beside me without another word.

"Thank you," I said quietly. I felt incapable of saying more than a few words at a time. How would I get through this testimony? And what was taking so long? They had insisted that I come right over, and now everything had paused.

After what seemed an eternal wait, an officer came out to meet us. He ushered us into a small holding room for a basic search.

What do they think I'm going to do?

From there, we wound our way back through the building.

"This is a confusing walk you're leading us on," I mentioned to the officer.

"No kidding," he said. "When I first started here, I got lost all the time."

Brian met us outside the door to the conference room, where the interview would take place.

"How are you?" he asked. "You okay?"

"I'm fine. I just want to get this over with."

We walked into the conference room. Two banquet-type tables sat end to end, and the police directed me to sit at the far end. Lynn and my attorney were asked to sit at the near end. As we walked in, another guy was taking a video camera out of a box and trying to set it up on a tripod.

Two gentlemen joined me at the opposite side of the table: Al, the lead detective from the township, and Peter, a corporal from the state police. Al sat at the head of the table, and Peter sat across from me. The officer fumbling with the video camera had trouble getting it to work, so we did quick introductions without the camera, just to expedite the process.

While the officer continued to wrestle with the camera, Al began to review the procedure.

"I'm going to be asking the questions," Al told me. "As we go along, I'll type the questions as well as your responses."

I can't believe this. Unless that guy types like crazy, we are going to be here all night. I won't make it through that!

He started the interview by typing the introduction and the first question. Al's typing skills were not what I had hoped for, and I felt even more serious concerns that I would not make it through hours and hours of this. We had barely started the interview when Peter requested that we stop for a moment.

Everyone, including my attorney, left the room. I remained seated, wondering what was going on.

Brian came back into the room.

"They've agreed to video tape your statement."

Al and Peter returned with another officer carrying a new box and a tripod, as well as a video disc recorder.

Great, let's get moving.

Unfortunately, it wasn't that simple.

I don't think they had ever used that kind of video recorder prior to my visit. It looked like the officer who had brought in the box was reading the instructions. I sat quietly. Lost in my own thoughts, conserving what little strength I had left. If I hadn't been there for such a serious purpose, the whole thing would have felt like a scene from an old TV comedy show. Finally, the recorder was ready, and we received the go ahead.

Al began by identifying all of the individuals present.

"This interview is being performed at the request of Tim Kreider. He has come to the police station on his own accord and at the direction of his attorney. This interview will be transferred to a typed statement for Mr. Kreider's review and approval."

"That's fine," I responded.

At last, we got started.

It was 7:05pm, and we were beginning the interview. Forty-five minutes away my three children were together, something that probably wouldn't happen again.

I should be there, I thought. *Not here.*

"Do you know the purpose of your visit here?"

"Yes, I do."

"And that purpose is?"

"To expose what I know regarding my son's involvement in the Haines' murders."

"And your son's name is?"

"Alec Kreider."

The enormity of the situation pressed down on my mind, my heart. This was it. I was turning in my beloved son for this horrible crime. It was really happening. I began to wring my hands as I spoke, something Lynn later told me I did through the entire interview. I focused all of my energy on answering the questions. I felt like my son's life and future were in my hands – I had to tell the truth, but perhaps somehow I could make a difference.

Perhaps if I let everyone know just how sick he is, that he needs help.

In retrospect, this line of thinking, and the self-imposed pressure that came with it, were futile. But at that time, I needed to believe that there was a possibility that I was helping my son. Otherwise, I was simply betraying him.

We covered Alec's age, birth date, the living arrangements of the boys, my address, his mother's name, our marital status, and when the divorce took place. I started getting frustrated – why did we need to go through all of those details?

What does any of this have to do with why I am here? This is taking too long. Let's get moving.

Later, Brian explained their line of questioning to me. The police followed a particular method of interrogation, a piece of which involved generating some rapport with the person being interviewed. They literally spent the first 15 to 30 minutes asking me things that had little or nothing to do with the case, and at the time, it nearly drove me crazy.

Occasionally, I looked over at Lynn and my attorney. They would both give me encouraging looks, a smile. Their presence gave me some comfort.

The questions continued: what about my daughter? Her name? Where did she live? Then back to the living arrangements of the kids: further clarification of where they stayed and how long that had been the case. Then, we moved on to Alec: how was school? What classes did he take? With what activities was he involved? Did he enjoy those activities? How were his grades? Did he miss much school? What classes did he like?

This became difficult for me to discuss – his hobbies? His interests? What did it matter? He'd never get to do them again! Alec was an excellent student: he was in the most advanced math class available, took any honors classes that he could and received straight A's. I couldn't remember the last time he missed school due to illness. He worked hard.

But none of it mattered any more. None of it! Why did I need to go over all of this? It made it all so much more painful! Couldn't we just get to the point of why I was there?

"How was he at home, this past year?" Al asked.

I told him the things that Alec and I spoke about. I explained what a good day looked like for Alec and how a bad day went. I explained how I always tried to get him to open up.

We moved on to his friends and classmates, and we discussed the girls who had befriended him. Then, we moved on to Kevin and his other best friend.

"When was the last time that Kevin was at your house?" he asked. "And what did the boys do?"

I couldn't remember the date. I should have been able to, but my brain couldn't come to grips with the passage of time. Anything prior to the last 30 days felt as if it had only existed in a dream. My frustration seeped through, but Al was patient.

Then, finally, Al began asking questions about the events of Saturday, May 12.

18

Revisiting Saturday

"Can you recount the events of Saturday, May 12?"

Having the benefit of hindsight, the events of May 12th took on greater significance. Everything seemed different.

At this point, Peter began interjecting questions – they were short, concise, and to the point. I appreciated that, because with each minute the stress, emotional exhaustion, and physical fatigue weighed heavier on me. I could barely sit up or focus on the questions any longer.

At one point, Al asked me a question and referred to Alec as Alex.

He should at least get that right by now.

But I answered the question and ignored the mistake. Suddenly, I heard Brian's voice:

"Alec. His name is Alec. A-L-E-C."

I glanced over at him and smiled – he was as frustrated as I at the line of questioning and how long it was taking. He was a father – he knew the strain I felt.

"How well did you know the Haines family?"

"Kevin and Alec were friends for five or six years. Kevin came to the house a lot. I was friendly with his father. He was an avid runner, and I have run off and on throughout my life, so we talked about that sometimes. Every once in a while, I'd see him running through the neighborhood. I can't say we were friends, but we were friendly and knew each other through our children."

Al spent a lot of time discussing the 12th – What had I noticed about Alec? What was he wearing? How long was I with him? What did Alec say? The questions went on and on. Once again, I found it difficult to maintain some kind of perspective on the passing of time.

"Alec's been up and down for a long time – he was stressed about his school work, both the amount and the grades. He complained about things and people that annoyed him or bothered him at school and in the news."

Peter spoke up.

"Has Alec spoken at all about what he wants to do after high school?"

"Alec was interested in law enforcement," I replied, the irony of my statement sinking in.

How did we end up here, in this building? How could Alec have done the things he claims to have done?

They asked more questions about Alec's recent mood.

"He spoke to me about various things. He didn't like the thoughts he was having – he wouldn't tell me what they were. Only that some of them scared him, and he didn't think I would understand. He told me there was something wrong with him, but he'd never go any further."

"What did you say to him?"

"I told him he should speak with a counselor, but he refused."

This is when I noticed that I was wringing my hands again, a nervous habit I picked up during that time and would do for years, especially when thinking back through those events. Sitting there at the table, struggling to recall the details they wanted and reliving the past months, it was difficult to maintain my composure. It began to wear on me, and I felt the onset of a headache. I couldn't concentrate.

"What about the events on the night that Alec's mother called the police?"

Alec and I had a conversation about that very subject at Philhaven, and I had forgotten about it until Al asked me that question.

"I asked Alec to be straight with me – would he have really killed himself that night? He said he had been thinking about it off and on for a long time. He promised the young lady on the phone that he wouldn't do it that night. We had planned a counseling appointment for that Friday, and he said he was going to open up about it then. He told me he was only playing with the gun, that he had chambered the bullet because he was interested in how guns work. He smiled and admitted it was a dumb thing to do. He told me he was ready to turn things around. That was a few days before his confession."

They asked me about Alec's employment. I didn't understand why we were talking about that or how it was relevant. Then, Peter interrupted, "We'll have to pause," he said. "The disc is full."

A complete disc's worth of material, and we haven't even gotten to why I'm here?

Part of me was happy for a break, but my greatest desire was to simply get this over with. I remained in my seat while they loaded a new DVD into the recorder, but something went wrong; the new disc didn't work. They tried another disc. It didn't work either. The minutes passed as they tried to find out why the recorder wasn't working. I was beginning to lose my patience. It was grueling to sit there as the time passed.

The whole scene began to get absurd.

"I have a camcorder at my house if that will help?"

My attorney smiled and shrugged as if he too found it unbelievable. I walked over to him, shaking my head.

"This is ridiculous," I said.

He did the best he could to calm my nerves. I could feel I was losing my ability to focus.

Eventually, they got their technical stuff worked out, and the interview continued. We finished a brief discussion of Alec's part-time jobs then switched back to his time in Philhaven.

"So," Al asked. "What happened at Philhaven that leads you to believe that Alec was involved with the Haines murders?"

I recounted our discussions at the family counseling sessions, the concerns over Alec not being discharged when he wanted and, also, about how he would handle the news about the young lady he was "in love" with. I relived that evening with them. I got to the time when Alec asked us to leave the room, but my headache distracted me.

This was it. It was time for me to talk about the reason I was there. The magnitude of what I was about to say sunk in – everything that I had said up to that point incriminated Alec (just my being there did that), but what I was about to say would give final proof of his involvement.

"Can I get some aspirin?" I asked.

While my attorney went to retrieve some medicine for me, the questioning turned to details of Alec's confession. I went through every detail that I could remember: what he wore, the knife he used, where he got it. What had Alec said about his feelings that night? The questions took on a redundant quality, revisiting the same details in the hopes that something else would come to my mind. But I faded quickly.

I was in disbelief. *Why was I telling the police all of these things about my son?*

The questioning turned to the memorial service, then back to the knife, then to the details Alec gave about the crime scene. Back to the ball cap, then to the flashlight. Back to the coat and how he left the house.

Wasn't this ever going to end? Why do we keep jumping all over the place?

"Do you believe Alec told you the truth?"

The truth.

"I had some fears about that after our first family counseling session. He's struggled with anger and dark thoughts. I tried to get him to open up, but he wouldn't tell me details."

I paused for a moment.

"There were times after the Haines family was murdered and before his confession, that I wondered if Alec had anything to do with it. But you never want to believe that your own child is capable of doing such things, especially not to a friend. It didn't make sense to me. It still doesn't."

Soon after that, Al asked me the last question of the day.

"Has Alec shown any remorse or said anything along those lines?"

"Alec said it doesn't seem real to him," I explained. "During one conversation he said, 'Mom, Dad – I can't believe I actually did this.'"

The men looked at each other; then, one of them turned to me.

"We appreciate that you came in willingly and talked to us about this."

That was it: the interview ended.

It was over! I didn't have to be strong any more. I leaned forward and put my forearms on the table, clasped my hands and bowed my head and just looked down. I was completely spent, distraught. I feared for Alec and the rest of my family. I felt guilty about missing the time with my kids that night and for turning in my son. I tried to gather strength enough to stand, just get up out of the chair.

I felt weak, alone and defeated.

When I finally looked up, Peter still sat across from me. He leaned forward with his arms on the table much as I did, looking directly at me. He had tears in his eyes. He felt my pain. By then, it was just him, Lynn, and me in the room.

"Do you blame yourself?"

"In some ways, yes," I replied. "If I could have been more insistent on Alec getting help, maybe this wouldn't have happened. I should have known. I am his father."

"No way," he said firmly. "There's no way you could have known."

He reached out to me, and his hands covered mine.

"This is not your fault," he continued. "You can't blame yourself."

I looked at him, fighting back a flood of emotions. Tears filled my eyes. I heard what he said but didn't believe it. I felt like I should have done more. So many lives ruined, and I knew I should have stopped it. Somehow. He didn't understand.

"Thanks," I said, slowly rising.

Lynn stood beside me. She had been there through it all – I looked at her, and she knew I was done. I had to leave. We left the room, and Peter walked us to the front doors of the police station.

"Tim, listen. This isn't your fault."

I still wasn't convinced.

"Thanks," I said.

"No, really, when I was young, I struggled with my father. I had anger issues, too. No one else could have done anything about what went on inside me. It was something I had to deal with on my own."

I listened, not saying anything.

"I've got a son," he continued. "I worry about him. It's not uncommon for teenage boys to fight with feelings of anger. Kids are angry these days."

Now, it made sense to me. Peter was a father, too, and tears filled his eyes.

"Alec made a very bad decision. You can't blame yourself for that."

The effort he made to reach out amazed me – it went well beyond his duty as an officer. When he finished, he gave me his business card.

"Call me if I can be of assistance in any way," he said. "If the media or anyone else harasses your family, call me, and I'll take care of it."

He made a huge difference in how I was feeling at that moment. He was a voice of compassion and not condemnation. I'll never forget his unexpected support and sincere kindness.

19

Conversations with Alec

My attorney came out of the building.

"I'd like to meet with you and Alec's mother tomorrow, just for a few minutes," he said. "As soon as your statement is typed, I'll let you know. You'll need to review and approve it. The details on how they are going to pick up Alec still need to be finalized – I'll be in touch if anything comes up that you need to know about." It was reassuring to have him on our side. Lynn and I thanked him; then, we got into the car and returned home. On our short ride to the house, I pictured the family members and friends I needed to tell. I didn't want them to discover this on the nightly news.

I called Chad first. He's one of my best friends and a former business partner, but I got his voice mail. I left a message, telling him to come over no matter what time.

Then, I tried reaching my supervisor, but I couldn't find her number. I didn't know who to talk to at work, so I called the president of the bank. I wanted him to be aware of the basic things that were going on so he could do what he thought was necessary to cover in my absence at the office – I didn't know what the fall out would be in the media.

"I'll probably be out for a few days," I said.

"Take as much time as you need. Take care of yourself and your family."

That was one less thing to worry about.

When I hung up, Lynn gave me a glass of water. I had hardly slept, eaten, or drank anything in days. I could tell she worried about me. I took the glass from her, and my hand immediately began shaking. I couldn't control it. I took a sip of water, and as I lowered the glass, the shaking continued. I put the glass on the counter. The shaking and lack of control bothered me; something so simple was beyond my strength.

My checklist for the day had been completed: everything that I could do up to that point had been done. I had spoken with the police, called my work, and contacted some key friends. I still had to let my side of the family know, but that could wait just a little longer. Right now, there was nothing left for me to do – I had been hanging on all day, keeping it together so that I could take care of what needed to be done, but now it was over, and I felt myself slipping.

I paced around the room, my mind darting here and there through the events of the previous days. I had been praying that Alec would get better. Then, I prayed that God not take my son from me. I had prayed that God would protect my family. None of my prayers seemed to matter: Alec's life was over, and my family would soon be exposed to the chaos and intrusion of the press. Why was this happening?

The Haines family, the terror they went through in the middle of the night, their daughter and what she saw and what she lost: thoughts about them consumed me. I felt responsible. I should have seen it coming. It was my fault. I failed as a father, and now three people were dead. A young woman lost her family, and the path of her life was now filled with unimaginable tragedy and pain. My son's life was destroyed. I would watch him grow up and turn into a young man, then enter middle age, all in prison. And he would watch from prison as I grew older and eventually died, leaving him alone. It was all gone. So many lives lost, altered, and damaged because of my failure as a father.

I wandered through the house, thoughts ravaging my mind. I felt weak. I found myself in the dining room and sat on the floor, leaning against the wall between the living room and the dining room. It was dark except for the light from the kitchen that flowed into where I was. I wept. How could this be happening? What did I do in my life to deserve this? I rolled over on to my side, curled up in the fetal position, facing the wall.

How would I get through this?

My faith was being tested. Until recently, I had wandered toward then away from God. Born and raised in Lancaster County, surrounded by a conservative community, I found it easy to question the idea of faith because of the hypocrites I often saw. I watched self-proclaimed religious people lie and cheat one another. Greed was commonplace. Most people were judgmental.

I called these people 1/7th Christians – on Sundays they were people of God, but on the other six days of the week, they followed their own self-serving desires. They used religion as a mask to cover their true selves. I turned away from the faith these people claimed to have.

But as my relationship with Lynn grew stronger, I began to once again explore faith and what it looked like to have a relationship with God. Lynn and some of her friends showed me a sincere and genuine effort to "practice what they preached." They were not perfect, just as none of us are, but their hearts reflected what they believed. I began to understand that the core of religion wasn't the problem – the problem was people who in their own weakness gave in to temptation. I realized I shouldn't judge Christianity as a whole based on the inappropriate actions of others, but that I needed to explore the Bible for myself and make a decision based on what it said and not how others behaved. The months leading up to now had become a time of significant spiritual growth for me, and my faith had grown much deeper.

God had come into my heart. I had changed as a person, turning away from the actions of my past. I was a new person, recognizing the hurt and pain I had caused my family, friends and partners because of my selfishness and disregard. I had moved away from that life of emptiness.

But at that moment, lying in the fetal position on the floor in the dining room, facing the wall, I could not see the light. I did not feel strong. I began to gently bump my head against the wall as I rocked back and forth.

"How can there be any good in this?" I muttered. "For Alec, for my family, for the Haines family, how can there be any good in this? God, I can't see it. Where is it? Where is the good in this?"

Lynn came over, sat down next to me, and tried to comfort me. I wanted the pain to go away. I wanted to wake up from this nightmare. I wanted things to go back to how they were before. But nothing would ever be how it was. All of our lives had been changed beyond imagination.

Then, the telephone rang.

Lynn answered the phone, then looked at me with a strange expression on her face.

"It's Alec," she said softly.

I had to pull myself together. Somehow, I rose up out of that emotional and physical position and put the phone to my ear.

"Hey, Alec," I said.

By the tone of his voice, I could tell he was frantic.

"The authorities called Philhaven! They know about the shoes!"

He suddenly knew he was in trouble. It wasn't going to go away. I felt a small amount of relief – he didn't know that I had told the police about his confession.

"Your attorney and I are doing everything we can for you," I said. "Don't talk to anyone. Do you hear me? Your mother and I are coming up tomorrow."

"I'm scared, dad. What's going to happen? What are they going to do?"

I wasn't prepared to have that conversation with my son at that point. I wasn't ready to tell him what I had done that day – I needed more time before getting into that.

"Alec, I love you, okay? No matter what. I'll always be here for you."

Soon after I hung up the telephone, it rang again. It was my friend Chad, returning my call from earlier in the evening. I spilled the news to him because I couldn't think of any other way of saying it. It was getting late, but he insisted on coming right over. I hung up the phone and lay back down on the floor. I needed rest.

Less than ten minutes later, he arrived. Chad's got a huge personality and a wide smile, but he wasn't smiling tonight. We were business partners for a long time, and I never knew him to mince words. His confidence and intelligence came through in our business world, in a good way.

When he came into the house, I don't even remember saying anything. There wasn't anything to say. Chad had known me for years, watched me raise my kids, walked with me through my divorce, and understood how important my children were to me. He had two boys of his own. As a father and my dear friend, he could feel my pain – I could see it on his face. He walked toward me and gave me a long hug.

Chad, Lynn, and I stood in the kitchen, and I leaned on the counter with one hand and tried to take a drink. My hand trembled, and I was still powerless to control it. I put the water down, not wanting him to see the depth of what I was experiencing. Lynn got Chad a beer.

He had so many questions. I gave him the basics of what had happened during the previous 48 hours, being careful not to tell him too much. I knew I could trust that Chad wouldn't share what I told him but didn't want to put him into a compromising position. He was a lot like me – if he hears about something concerning a loved one, he wants to help fix it, take care of it. Here was a situation that neither of us could do anything about. The damage had been done.

But one small exchange of dialog stands out in my mind: he had always taken a very strong stance on the death penalty, saying that if you take a life you should get the death penalty.

"Do you still agree with a 'mandatory' death penalty?" I asked with a wry smile. It was a poor attempt at humor. It's one of my flaws: ill-timed humor.

He gave me an "Oh, man" look.

"I probably have a different opinion on it now," he admitted.

My own opinions on various things would change quite a bit after this experience. It's amazing how our perspectives can shift when we experience things for ourselves. There are many sides to every situation. Taking the time to consider and understand all points of view opens our mind to possibilities we may never have considered based only on our own experiences.

It was pushing midnight, and I started to fade. Chad gave me another hug before leaving. Then, it was just Lynn and me. It was late. Before bed, we prayed for Alec, the Haines family, and our family. We all needed God's grace and help.

As usual, I couldn't sleep. All of the emotions, fear, doubt, guilt, anger, pain, and loss overwhelmed me. I tormented myself again about my role in the situation. I should have forced Alec to get help. I should have been a better spiritual leader for my family – having faith may have helped Alec in his fight against his illness, given him strength to reach out.

I looked at every aspect of my history as Alec's father and the influence I had on him. Every time I had lost my temper or had been a poor role model festered in my mind. Alec had always had a difficult temperament, but I had carried my own issues into adulthood, and that made it tough for me to know how to respond to Alec's anger.

It had taken me many years to come to terms with my own anger. Unfortunately, during Alec's childhood, I often responded to him in anger in an effort to "control" his behavior and get him to "listen."

Had I been the early role model that set him on this path?

Did he learn to lash out in anger from me?

Did the way I treated him create the emotional turmoil and angst Alec now had to endure?

My inability to control my emotions and actions was responsible for all of it. If I had better understood how to respond in love and patience, perhaps things would have turned out very differently. I had failed my son and my family. My past weaknesses, doubt, and lack of conviction had put us in this situation. All I had ever wanted was to love my children, be a good father, and take care of them. But three words kept echoing in my mind.

I had failed.

I had failed.

20

The Strength For One More Day

It was the worst night of my life. I contemplated all that I had done and didn't do as a father, what I could and should have done, and how different all of our futures would now be if I had. I thought about how my lack of ability would affect my children and Lynn. Everything tumbled over and over in my mind.

The morning sun came through the bedroom window. I'm not sure if I even slept that night.. I stared up at the ceiling. I couldn't move. The mental, emotional, and physical fatigue was complete. The lack of sleep or food in the previous 60 hours, combined with stress and emotional trauma, had taken an extreme toll on me.

Lynn reached over for my hand. I couldn't move it – I didn't have an ounce of strength. I didn't even want to turn my head.

"How are you this morning?" she asked me.

"I don't have the strength to get out of bed," I whispered. "I've got nothing left."

I started to cry: for Alec, for the Haines family, for Lynn and my other two children. I cried for myself. There was no hope. No reason to get up and go on. I knew that my attorney would bring the typed testimony over for me to review. I knew we needed to discuss what was coming down the road. Soon, the time would come for me to visit Alec, explain to him what

I had done and why. The authorities would probably want to come to search the house again.

How was I going to do it? I didn't have the luxury of breaking down or losing it. Too many things demanded my attention. No one else could do everything that was required to support and protect Alec. It was up to me. But the strain of this extreme experience had beaten me.

Lynn squeezed my hand. I didn't even have the energy to squeeze her hand back. The most I could do was eventually turn my face towards her. I couldn't focus my thoughts or energy. I didn't want to move, even if I could. I didn't want to face anything else.

I was finished.

Through the years leading up to that point, I had read many self-help books by some of the greatest minds in the world. They helped me struggle through the difficulties in my life: becoming a father at 20 years old, working three jobs on my way through college, financial shortfalls, family conflicts, career uncertainty, and then the experience of divorce. I always tried to find the upside.

Talk to any of my co-workers or friends – they would tell you I've always been extremely positive. I did my best to live by the philosophy that I could not control anything in life except for what I think, feel, do, and believe. When I first understood this reality, it was a sobering thought. I felt helpless in a world where I had no control. But then it hit me. I have control of the most important thing there is in life. My self! No matter what others may think or do, I was always in control of how I reacted, what I thought, what I believed, and what I did. It was a long process, but I knew that my response was up to me. Events don't control what we think and feel – it is up to us to determine how we react to what happens.

But at that moment, lying in my bed, none of that mattered. No amount of positive self-help talk could move me in spite of everything that I had read. Never before had I felt so low and weak. It was the first time in my life that I threw in the towel, where I admitted I couldn't do it. I was too drained. It was hopeless. There was no way I could get out of that bed.

I wasn't even able to squeeze Lynn's hand! Who was I kidding? What was I going to do? I just kept crying and felt like giving up. Someone else would have to do everything for me. I had nothing. I was nothing. All of the fear, pain, and guilt that enveloped me weighed much more than I could carry. I just wanted it to go away – how could I make it go away?

I stared up at the ceiling. No energy, no will to move, no hope. Lynn held my hand and looked at me, but there was nothing she could do. There was nothing anyone else could do. I had never felt more alone or helpless in my life – not during my childhood, not during my divorce, not even when Alec went into Philhaven. This was the bottom.

Then a thought came into my head.

I'm not alone.

"Jesus, I need the strength for one more day," I whispered. "I need the strength for me and my family, just one more day. Give me the strength."

I lost myself in prayer. I don't know how many times I prayed that simple prayer, but I kept on. Strength was available to me, far greater than anything I brought to the table on my own. I wasn't much of a pray-out loud kind of person, but the words spilled out of my mouth.

"Please give me strength for today, to do the things I have to do. My family, my son, they need me. Just help me get through today. Amen."

I closed my eyes. What happened next is difficult to explain.

A tingling sensation started in my cheeks, first barely there but then stronger until my entire face tingled. The feeling moved over my head then traveled throughout my body, moving down my chest and arms and into my legs. Soon my whole body was consumed by this strange sensation.

I began shaking all over.

"I don't know why I'm shaking," I told Lynn. "I'm not cold."

"It's okay," she said. She knew what was happening to me. She let go of my hand.

I lifted my hands toward the ceiling, palms facing up. I don't know how long the sensation lasted: just a moment? A few seconds? A few minutes? It doesn't matter. All I know is that once the sensation subsided, I felt rejuvenated and revitalized. I no longer felt drained of my energy or incapable of dealing with what faced me.

"Thank you, Jesus. I believe."

Almost instantly the tingling and shaking flashed over my entire body again.

Strength had returned to my body. The fog in my mind disappeared. The guilt and hopelessness were gone. I got out of bed, amazed and thankful. I looked at Lynn.

"Now, I can go help my son," I proclaimed, overwhelmed by a calm feeling of purpose. Lynn stared at me in amazement, tears welling in her eyes with the hint of a smile.

Whatever I have to do today, I will be able to do it, I thought.

I took a shower, preparing for the meeting with our attorney later that morning. The hot water ran down over my head and body. I felt so thankful for the newfound strength and peace. For the first time in weeks, I felt relaxed – where had all the pain and anguish gone? As I stood there, enjoying the simple pleasure of standing up, a thought thrust into my head. It was an idea that would change the direction and purpose of my life.

Start an outreach to the teenagers of our country.

I was supposed to take this experience with my son, the gifts given to me, and begin a movement to help young people.

Less than twelve hours before, I had been curled up, lying on the floor in my dining room, asking God how anything good could ever come of this experience. Now, I was being told exactly what my role would be in turning the event into something positive. How and why had this thought come to me? Up until that moment, I hadn't been concerned for the welfare of anyone except Alec, my family, and the Haines family. Yet, a new and wonderful vision entered my mind in the midst of the most horrible circumstances.

The idea exhilarated me. I got out of the shower, wrapped a towel around myself, and practically ran downstairs to the kitchen. Lynn was making her coffee.

"I know what I'm supposed to do now," I exclaimed.

"Tim! You're dripping wet!" Lynn said, laughing and slightly alarmed.

I realized I hadn't even toweled off.

"It doesn't matter. I know what I'm going to do with the rest of my life."

I told her about the idea of using this event as a catalyst to help teenagers that faced some of the challenges that Alec had faced. We both got excited about the possibilities.

This situation can be turned around. Help and hope for others will come out of this. Focus on today's tasks, but a seed has been planted.

I returned to the bathroom, shaved, and got dressed in slacks and a dress shirt. It was the first time in days I had done any of those things. The tasks at hand and the situation in total no longer felt overwhelming. I now had the strength to do what needed to be done and then some.

That morning, Diane and I met with our attorney.

"You look good," Brian said, sounding mildly surprised. "Are you okay? You don't have to dress up for me, you know."

I smiled.

"I'm feeling much better this morning. Some day, I'll tell you about it."

He reviewed with us the steps that would happen next.

"The authorities are going to pick up Alec from Philhaven on Saturday. They're not sure on the time yet, but they're thinking around noon. You'll need to stop by the municipal office today as soon as the statement is transcribed."

I nodded.

"Review it," he continued, "Make any corrections, then sign it."

"What about seeing Alec?" Diane asked.

"You can visit Alec today at Philhaven, but there will be a state police officer present. He'll be in plain clothes – most of the staff at Philhaven are not aware of the situation, so you need to keep it to yourselves."

"And on Saturday?" I asked. "How will the pick-up work?"

"He'll be taken quietly," he said in a serious voice. "We're doing everything we can to keep the press out of the picture for as long as possible. He'll be taken to the District Magistrate's office for arraignment then sent to the Manheim Township police for processing. Once that's complete, he'll be sent to the Lancaster County Prison, where he'll stay until his fate is determined."

The Lancaster County Prison. My boy, my Alec, would be going to prison. Alone.

"There is no chance of bail," our attorney said.

I nodded. I hadn't expected any.

"Right now, I'm arranging one last meeting for you to have with Alec at the police station prior to him being taken to prison."

"Thank you," I said. He nodded. He had thought of everything, wanting the process to run as smoothly as possible.

"Listen. By the time Alec gets to the township building, word will have gotten out. The press will be there. Someone needs to make a statement."

"I'll do it," I said quickly. "I'll take responsibility for that."

He shook his head.

"I don't think that's a good idea. Let me handle it – your role in the arrest and the fact that you are Alec's father complicate things. It will be very intense. I don't want you facing the barrage of questions or the frenzy this is going to cause."

Part of me still felt that it was my responsibility, but I agreed with him. It would be like nothing I had ever experienced, and he was familiar with the press, what to say and what not to say. He could control the event. Once we agreed to this, I felt a great sense of relief. I had dreaded giving a statement. We've all seen that end badly too many times on TV.

Diane and I stood to leave, and Brian gave us a few last minute instructions.

"I'll be in contact with you on Saturday once we know the time that Alec will be picked up. That way you can get there before the press finds out. After that, it will be chaos."

Our attorney did everything in his power to protect my family and me, and for that, I am eternally grateful.

Diane and I drove to Philhaven. They permitted us to have an earlier meeting time due to the circumstances. I looked forward to seeing Alec but wasn't looking forward to explaining to him what I had done. I wasn't sure what to expect.

21

Telling Alec

"I have something I want to talk to you about, Alec," I said.

The three of us – Alec, his mother, and I – returned to the same small room in Philhaven, a place I was beginning to feel familiar with. Alec sat with his back facing the far wall, and I sat directly across from him, my back to the door. His mother was to my right. For a few moments after I said that sentence we all waited, sitting around the table, not saying anything. I didn't know how to begin.

Well, here goes, I thought to myself.

"I went to the police last night, Alec. I gave them a statement about what you told your mother and I on Tuesday. It was the only thing I could do to give you a chance – eventually, the authorities would have put things together on their own. They would have figured it out. Because I went to them, we were able to get 2nd degree murder removed, which gives us the possibility of a mental health defense."

For a moment, silence settled on the room. Then, I continued.

"Without this option, there would be no hope of you getting any sentence other than life."

Diane stared at him, waiting for his response. Then, he spoke, and his voice was soft.

"I understand, Dad. My attorney spoke to me earlier and explained what was happening. He told me why you did what you did. I'm fine with it."

Relief washed over me. I wasn't going to lose my relationship with my son! He didn't hate me.

We discussed what would happen next and what his future would most likely look like. I didn't want to talk about it much because it was too early to know the direction things would go, and the worst-case scenario felt too possible and too painful to consider. I found it difficult to keep a strong and positive facade while talking about the possibility of Alec spending the rest of his life behind bars.

For the first time, Alec absorbed the severity of the situation. He realized there was no way out. He began to take rapid, deep breaths. I thought he was going to hyperventilate. He stared down at the table, but I saw the anxiety and fear spreading on his face. What all of this meant for his future was something I struggled to come to terms with – it was obvious that he was now beginning to consider the same questions.

The life he had expected was over. At 16, he should have had his entire life to look forward to. How can anyone, at that age, even begin to understand and accept that, for the rest of his life, he will be in prison? I walked around the small table and put my arms around Alec, pulled his head against my chest. I couldn't do anything else. I just held on, talked to him softly, and told him I loved him.

Slowly, his breathing began to calm. I let go of him and returned to my seat.

"So what's next?" he murmured.

"The police will come on Saturday. We don't know the details yet."

"How long will I be in prison? Where will I end up?"

"The recommended sentence for 3rd degree murder is 6 – 40 years per count with the chance of parole. 1st degree murder is life in prison without parole. Our best chance of a lesser sentence would be with the mental health defense. It's too early to know for sure."

I found it difficult to believe that I was having this conversation with my 16-year-old son. Alec began breathing heavily again. This time, his mother moved closer, leaning forward and putting her arm around his shoulder. They both rested there, on the table, and Alec slid his arm around his mom. I grabbed on to his arm with both hands and prayed that he would have peace and strength to face what was in front of him.

Slowly, he calmed down again. Our visit lasted for a few more minutes.

"We're going to go, Alec. But we'll be back later today."

Once I was home I called Brian.

"Anything new with the statement?"

"It's still not ready for your review. The transcription process is taking them longer than expected, and some parts of the video aren't clear. I'll let you know when it's ready."

I did a few things around the house and got ready to head back to Philhaven. Before we had left that morning, the staff told us we could bring in a meal for Alec and have dinner with him. Diane had asked him what he wanted to eat, and he picked Chinese food, one of his favorites. So we headed to Philhaven that night, Chinese food in hand.

They gave us the same room, which allowed us to have a semi-private meal together. I recognized the state police officer immediately – he was clean-cut and carried a much more serious air about him than the regular Philhaven staff. His face was somehow familiar to me, but I couldn't place him.

Alec, his mother, and I sat at the small table and shared a meal of Chinese food and egg rolls. Alec enjoyed the food a great deal, and I was astonished at how well he was holding it together. He was very aware that this might be the last time he got to eat Chinese food from his favorite restaurant.

It was difficult for me to sit and watch him enjoy such a simple pleasure, knowing he would most likely never have it again. My heart ached for him, for us. I felt sick for all that had been lost.

When we finished eating, Alec handed me something.

"Here, Dad, this is for you."

It was a Father's Day card. He had made me a Father's Day card. Suddenly, I realized that Father's Day was only two days away. I had forgotten and was deeply touched that in the midst of all that chaos he had remembered.

He had made the card out of yellow construction paper. On the front, it read "Happy Father's Day," and he had drawn the sun, a tree, and some flowers. I opened it:

Forever has your love for me comforted me through good times and bad. Forever will I need your love and support to make it to a new, brighter day. Your loving son, Alec

I wept. How could this be happening to my boy? He handed me a drawing of a flower, created from memory, one of his best sketches ever. My heart was a wreck – the beauty and tragedy of that moment is hard to explain. My son still loved me and needed me. The last few days had not destroyed our relationship. Why did it take this experience for him to get it? Where would all of this lead us?

Once I composed myself, we turned our attention to a few housekeeping issues. We had brought in his paychecks from work – I told him to sign them over to me so that I could deposit them into his account. He then wrote a check out to me so that I could deposit his money, the little that it was, in a better place.

"Here, you sign your checks on the back. Yeah, right there. Now, to write out a check you put the date there, the amount there. That's right."

This would become one of the most piercing memories for me: it shined a spotlight on what I was losing. It ripped my heart out. I thought I'd have plenty of time to teach him these basic life skills, but now he probably would never need to write another check.

"What are we going to do about my savings account?" Alec asked.

"I don't think there's that much money in there," I replied.

"There's at least $100!" he exclaimed.

I could tell it was a big deal to him. $100. He went back to the task of endorsing his checks, but the comment about the money was a terrible blow for me. Everything that happened in that little room magnified the losses and absurdity of our lives at that moment. A hundred dollars was nothing compared to what his future cost, yet it was so very important to him. He had so much growing up to do and life to experience. But now it didn't matter! I'd never teach him how to drive, show him what to do with his money, or go on college visits with him. I'd never take him for a hair cut again or watch movies with him or simply watch him grow into a man. I knew that once this came out, everyone would look at him as some kind of monster. But to me, he was still my little boy.

I thought of the same thing for the Haines family – all the things that their daughter would not be able to experience because of what Alec had done. It was overwhelming, thinking of all that would not be, not just for Alec and myself, but for everyone involved.

"I'll take care of your money," I said. "You might need it some day."

We clung to that speck of hope.

"Do you want me to be here on Saturday when the police come to pick you up?" I asked.

He thought about it for a minute.

"I don't think you should," he said. "It will be harder for me if you guys are here."

His mother and I nodded. I felt slightly relieved — I would have been there if he wanted me to be, but I respected his show of concern for us. As we continued to talk, there was an air of inevitability, of finality, yet we weren't somber. We enjoyed our time together and wondered about the changes looming just over the horizon, painfully aware of how we couldn't keep them from coming.

The time came for us to leave. The three of us got up and walked out of the room. The state police officer and two staff members stood just outside the door, so we stopped right there to say good-bye.

Diane went first, tears streaming down her face. She wasn't crying audibly, but her pain and emotion covered all of us like breaking waves, drew us in like the undertow in the ocean.

"I love you, Alec," she said, holding him in an embrace. The three policemen assigned to Alec became visibly uncomfortable — it was a heart-breaking, personal moment, and I think they wished they weren't there. They glanced away, then back again, waiting for mother and son to end their embrace.

But Alec continued hugging his mother as if they both knew that once they released each other, that was it. It would be over. The men could no longer watch. They looked away. The hug went on and on. The orderlies were also feeling intrusive on this intimate family moment, shifting their weight and looking nervously around.

That last moment between a mother and her son, neither one wanting to let go: it was too painful to watch. A mother wishing she could change things, protect her son, and the boy wishing she could make it all go away, make it all better. It became difficult for even me to watch. Everyone in that space was drawn into their emotion and this sense that, after their embrace, everything would change. For the three of us, it was a significant breaking.

When they finally pulled apart, there was no going back. Alec's old life as an innocent troubled teen ended in that moment, and he began the process awaiting him.

It felt like his life was over.

I walked up to Alec.

"I'll always be here for you. I love you."

I hugged him.

"Be strong," I whispered into his ear. I didn't want to let go either, but I knew it was too late. There was nothing more I could do for him that night.

The staff members gave us Alec's bag with all of his clothing and personal items, the last remnants of a normal life. He wouldn't need them any longer.

22

Spreading the Word

When I arrived home that night, there were two phone calls I needed to make. I had put them off as long as possible. My father, as well as the rest of my extended family, still didn't know what was going on. How do you tell your father something like this about his grandson?

I called him, and we made small talk for a few minutes.

"I have something to tell you – there's no easy way to say this. Alec confessed to the Haines family murders."

He was silent. My father was not an emotional person, and I didn't try to draw him into a long conversation.

"Can you let the rest of the family know?" I asked him quietly.

"I'll call everyone tonight," he said.

After another moment of silence, we said good-bye.

Well, that's finished.

I had one more call to make that night, to a friend of mine who had been with me during some challenging times in my life. She had always been a great source of encouragement and faith. She knew how important my children were to me and how hard I had worked over the years to be a good father.

When I told her the news, she was obviously shaken, and the sorrow she felt for me and my family was clear. I was sure she would be a powerful support for me in the coming weeks.

After that, I knew I needed to get some rest. The next day, Saturday, would be another eventful one. I felt a certain level of acceptance taking over my emotions and demeanor: the course had been set and could no longer be changed. But there were still things I needed to do. I wanted to tell some people close to us, before they heard it in the news: what would their reaction be toward Alec, my family and me?

I slept well that night, and when I woke up the next morning, there was no promise of an easier or brighter day, but thankfully the peace and power of the day before remained with me. So much needed to happen in the next few hours: I had several difficult conversations ahead, and I had yet to receive the copy of my statement for review. Alec would be picked up and charged. I had no idea what to expect once this news hit the media.

The first task at hand was to talk to Alec's other best friend, the third of the "three musketeers." When Kevin was murdered, now just over a month ago, this young man had lost one of his best friends. Now, I was going to tell him that his other best friend was the one who did it. I had spoken with him and his mother at the Haines family memorial service; he had been at our house once to hang out with Alec; and I had checked in on him and his mother a few times during that difficult month.

I had told them that he could come over any time, and she had told me that he was having an extremely difficult time since Kevin's death. Finding out about Alec's involvement was sure to make it worse – I wanted him to find out from me. Not the media. Not the neighbors. I felt I owed it to him.

I waited to go to their house until 9:00am, hoping not to wake anyone. The drive only took about five minutes, but I found myself caught off-guard by the emotions that started to swell inside of me on my way there. I also realized how little time I had to prepare for this talk. I arrived at their house and pulled into the driveway, then sat there, collecting my thoughts. This was going to be a very difficult conversation. I didn't know where to begin.

Sitting here isn't helping anyone, I thought, slowly getting out of the car. I looked down the sloping driveway, into the street, and at the large trees in the front yard. Birds sang, and the sun felt warm – it looked like it would be a beautiful summer morning. How calm and tranquil! My gaze turned to the house. It was quiet. A foreboding rose inside of me - I didn't want to do it.

What was the difference? Why should I put myself through that? They would find out on their own, soon enough, without me delivering the news. But I gathered my resolve, closed my car door, and walked up the driveway to the steps that led up to the front door. I felt like I had no choice. Their family deserved to hear this news in person. It was the right thing to do.

I reached out, rang the doorbell, and waited. Their dog barked, but besides that, I didn't hear anything. I rang the doorbell again. The dog's barking became more frantic and loud.

Well, if they're home, that should wake them.

My anxiety was building. Through the window, I saw someone come down the stairs. I realized it was the younger sister – the same girl that had been so distraught at the memorial service. She opened the door and recognized me immediately.

"Hi, Mr. Kreider."

"Hi, I'm sorry I woke you up."

In spite of being jolted out of bed on a Saturday morning, she was her usual pleasant self.

"Is your mother home?" I asked.

"Yeah, but she's still sleeping."

"I have something important to talk to her about. Would you mind getting her for me?"

"Sure," she said, heading back up the stairs. I heard her voice shout down the hall.

"Mom! Alec's dad is here! He wants to talk to you!" She said this with the familiarity and friendliness of a time that no longer existed. A time of innocence and hope that had been taken away from all of us.

Eventually, the girl came back down.

"Mom will be down in a few minutes."

I didn't have to wait long.

"Hello, Tim," she said.

"Good morning."

I could tell she was curious as to what brought me there alone so early on a Saturday morning. We walked into the dining room so that we wouldn't be overheard. I didn't want her daughter hearing our conversation. I didn't know any other way to tell her about Alec, so I went with the direct approach.

"Today, Alec is going to be charged with the murders of Kevin and his parents."

She looked at me, trying to get her mind around that news.

"How...how are you doing?" she asked.

How thoughtful that she would think of me.

"I'm doing fine," I said, though it wasn't totally the truth. She asked a lot of questions. I shared with her what I could, but there was so much I couldn't tell her at the time.

"I'd like to tell your son personally, if that's okay."

She agreed.

"Why don't you wait out on the screened porch while I go wake him up?" she suggested.

I sat out in the screened porch while she went to get her son. Alone for a few minutes, just me and my thoughts, I wondered how my news would impact this family? For a moment, I envisioned the ripple effect that Alec's actions would bring about. Where would this stop? How many lives would be devastated by these events?

A minute or two later, she came out with her son and, seeing him, I second-guessed my decision. What a way for him to start the day. It was so unfair, like many other things that had taken place in the last month.

"Mr. Kreider has something he'd like to talk to you about," she said. He looked at me, his eyes searching mine, *What's going on?*

I thought about what a pleasant, respectful young man he was and what a pleasure it had been to have him in my house. He had grown up so much since we first met – he had gotten taller than me this past year and was well on his way to being a young man.

I can't believe what I have to tell him.

"Good morning," I said. "How are you? I'm sorry to wake you up."

He knew something was up.

"Alec is going to be charged today with the murders of Kevin and his parents."

129

There, I said it. He looked at me, not saying anything. Then, he glanced down at the ground.

"If there is anything else that I can do," I said quietly, "please let me know."

The three of us didn't talk long. Soon, he went back up to his room, and his mother and I sat there on that quiet summer morning.

"He'll be okay," she said. "I think we'll head out of town for a few days. It's going to get crazy around here."

"If you can get away, I'd do it," I said.

"I'm worried about you and your family, Tim. Do you have anywhere to go?"

"There's too much to do," I said with a sad smile. "But if things get too bad, I can get away."

I stood up to leave. She hugged me.

"Good luck," she said, concern on her face.

From there, I went to Drew's best friend's house. Ever since this had begun, I worried about my 12-year-old son, my youngest, wondering how this would affect the rest of his life.

I rang the doorbell, and his friend's mother came to the door.

"Do you mind if I come in? There's something I need to talk to you about," I said. It was definitely an unexpected visit, but she invited me in, and we sat down in the living room. I went straight to the reason for my visit, not seeing the point in small talk.

"My oldest son, Alec, is going to be charged with the Haines family murders later today," I said. "I hope this doesn't change anything regarding your son's friendship with Drew. Your family has been very important to him, and he's going to need his friends more than ever in the coming weeks and months."

"Tim, Drew is always welcome here," she said. "That's not going to change. He's a good boy and a joy to have around. Don't worry about that. If you need anything, let me know."

I explained that I wanted to go to my youngest son's other close friend and tell his parents as well.

"They're away on vacation," she said, "but I can tell them as soon as they get back if you'd like."

I nodded, pausing, I looked at the floor for a moment.

"Thank you so much."

A few days later I received a hand-written note from her in the mail that brought tears to my eyes. It would be the first of many such notes of support and prayers from our friends, family, and the general community. The Bible verse on the outside of the card was, "Do not fear: I will help you" Isaiah 41:13.

Inside the card. she wrote:

Dear Tim

Forgive me for not responding a whole lot to what you had to say to me on Saturday. It only sank in as you were walking away. As I watched you leave, I just wanted to hug you and tell you it will be okay. My heart was so grieved by all this. I couldn't help but cry and weep for you and your family. The unimaginable pain you must feel. But I want to say you are a great man of character. It took an incredible amount of courage for you to come to me with this news. I want you to know I hold you in the highest respect. You are a good man. My heart goes out to you and your children, including Alec. I will be praying for you. If you need someone to talk to, we are here for you. I don't have a lot of answers, but I have an ear to listen. God bless you and tenderly give you comfort, refresh you with his grace, and by His strength protect you.

I started sobbing when I first read it, and to this day, that note makes me cry. She is a busy woman with five children, a husband, and a job; she has a lot going on, and the fact that she took the time to send me those words of encouragement reassured me that confiding in her was the right thing to do.

I returned home exhausted emotionally, but I had one final call to make, to my mother. She lived in Maine, so I knew she wasn't getting a lot of the same information we got at the local level, but I assumed this would make national news. I needed to let her know about it before it traveled across the country. I called her on her cell but had to leave a message.

"Hey, Mom, call me as soon as you get this. I need to talk to you right away."

Later in the morning, I waited at my house. I waited to hear that my typed statement was ready for me to review. I waited for news on when the authorities would pick up Alec from Philhaven. I waited to hear any further news from my attorney. The waiting was excruciating. I just wanted the day to end.

At noon, I received a call from the Manheim Township police station: my statement was ready. I arrived at the same waiting area and sat down. I saw the same reward sign, posted on the bulletin board. This time, I took it down and crumpled it up in a ball, held on to it. It was too painful to look at, and in my mind, there certainly wasn't a need for it any longer. Hadn't I given them enough?

"Mr. Kreider?" an officer asked, entering the lobby.

I stood up.

"Your statement has been typed. You need to review each page, initial them, and make any corrections."

I handed the officer the crumbled up reward notice.

"I don't think we need this any longer. It's the reward poster from the lobby," I explained.

His expression went from one of bewilderment to apology.

"I'll get rid of it for you."

He took me to another room and handed me my statement typed in a two-page summary as well as a 54-page document of everything I said on Thursday night. As I sat down and began reviewing the statement, I had flashbacks to that night. I relived it.

When I finally reached the section where I provided the incriminating details about Alec, it became difficult to see my own words in print. In my mind, it magnified what I had done. Feelings of guilt, betrayal, and remorse pushed their way into my heart and mind. It took all of my strength to focus on the lengthy document and complete the task.

Read one line at a time, and push through it, I told myself.

Relief flooded over me as I turned to the last page. It was finished.

I went home and waited for the call. Soon, they would be picking up Alec and taking him into custody.

23

Alec's Arrest and Father's Day

The time the authorities were going to pick up Alec changed as the day went on. Then my attorney called and said it would still be sometime that day, but the time wasn't set. Everything started to remind me of the chaos on the night I gave my statement. The constant delays felt excruciating.

Sometime in the middle of the afternoon, the phone rang – it was my mother. We chatted briefly, and there wasn't an easy way to tell her what had happened in the past few days.

"Have you heard of the Haines family murders?" I asked her. When she wasn't sure, I gave her some of the details, and then, she said she remembered hearing about it from some of her friends.

"Alec is going to be charged with that crime," I said quietly.

She became distraught.

"Should I come stay with you guys?" she asked.

"It's up to you," I said, and we decided she would come down later that evening.

Now that my family knew, it gave me time to sit back and reflect on what this meant for everyone and how our worlds were about to change. How would the media respond? Would my other children be punished by the community for their brother's transgressions? Could my youngest son go back to his school? Would those looking to publicize or sensationalize the story intrude into our lives?

Late in the afternoon, I got the call. The police were on their way to Philhaven to pick up Alec. They planned on taking him to the District Justice's office to have the charges filed. Meanwhile, the D.A. scheduled the press conference at the police station at the same time as the arraignment in an attempt to keep the media at bay, at least for now. My attorney also managed to arrange one last meeting between Alec and us at the police station.

Diane and I drove to the police station together, and when we arrived, we saw a media van parked out front. The word was out. I thought the circus was about to begin.

The police allowed Diane and me to park inside the garage at the back of the building – this would enable us to leave discreetly after our meeting with Alec, an unexpected favor and one I appreciated. After parking and going inside, we were led to a small room with a table and two chairs. We waited.

The two of us sat there, quietly. We didn't talk – there didn't seem to be anything to say. The officers gave us a pitcher of water and checked in on us occasionally. It was an uncomfortable time – the last few days had emptied and exhausted us.

Brian stopped by to check on us.

"I'll handle the statement for the family. Don't worry about it," he said.

I was glad he was there. Then, an officer leaned his head around the door.

"Alec is in the building. He'll be with you soon. He hasn't eaten for a while. What can we get for him? It needs to be something close and fast."

We decided on a sub – he could eat in the room and spend some time with us before being sent to prison. Finally, they instructed us that he was ready, and they led us to a different room.

Alec wore wrist and ankle shackles. This was a sight I never could have imagined. He shuffled into the room, accompanied by three officers. They remained there with us, only two or three paces away, which made conversation awkward. His food arrived, and we chatted about nothing in particular. Again, there didn't seem like much to say at that point. It's an odd thing, having a conversation with your son while he is shackled, knowing that in just a few minutes he will be taken away to prison, most likely for life. We had already said our good-byes the night before, and now things felt final. We all knew what was coming.

The visit was short, just long enough for Alec to finish his sandwich.

"It's time," one of the officers said.

I gave my son a hug, and then he was gone.

The local police told us they would be placing an officer in front of both of our homes for at least the next 48 hours to control the media and anyone else who might be curious. Unfortunately, I didn't believe this whirlwind would die down in two days, but it was comforting to know the police would be watching to keep unwelcomed visitors at bay. Diane and I left quietly through the back door. We could see the media vans lined up in front of the building. This was it – the news about my son was going out to the world.

I had no idea what to expect.

As I turned onto my street, I saw a police cruiser sitting across from my house and numerous other vehicles lined up just down the street on both sides. *Someone must be having a party,* I thought to myself. Then, I saw the people beside the vehicles and realized it wasn't a party; it was the press.

As long as they stay right there, that's fine with me, I thought. I had no desire to speak with them. They could sit there as long as they liked. I pulled into the garage, and Diane and I went inside. Lynn and Amy were waiting for us, and Drew was away at a friend's house. It seemed best for him to be away from any chaos that might occur once this hit the airways. If he could be spared the trauma of this situation, perhaps the long-term effects would be minimal. He'd have a chance at a "normal" life some day.

"You guys should spend the night here," I suggested to my daughter and her mom. "It might be better if we're all together for this."

But they didn't think it was necessary. They assured us they would be fine, so they went home, leaving Lynn and me alone. As they pulled out of the driveway, I noticed five or six neighbors gathered in the front yard next door.

I went back inside, looking for Lynn. She was out on the back patio with a glass of wine.

"Well, it's started," I said. "There's a group of neighbors in the yard next door – I've never seen anything like that before. Do you think we should join them?"

"Absolutely!" she said, standing up. "Let's go say hi." We held hands and walked around the side of the house to the small group.

Before we could say anything, one of the neighbors reached out and put her arms around Lynn, giving her a huge hug. Lynn was surprised – she had never met her before.

"We're here if you need us," the neighbor said. "If there's anything we can do, just let me know."

They offered to make us dinner and invited us to their house if we needed to get away. One neighbor gave us an open invitation to their swimming pool. The overwhelming support was incredible and more comforting than anything we had hoped for. But it was just the beginning of a huge wave of support our community would show us.

The most important part of the conversation came when everyone, without me asking, affirmed that they were not going to talk to the press or let them park in front of their homes. My neighbors on both sides and all three on the other side of the street did not want anything to do with the media. We were surrounded by caring people who would protect us by building a fortress of privacy around us. This gesture deeply touched me.

Lynn and I went back to the patio, and while we were walking, Lynn told me that a golfing friend of hers had called to say the network had broken into coverage of the U.S. Open Golf Tournament to announce what was going on with Alec and the case surrounding the Haines murders. In late April, this friend had been to our house to help us plant gardens as her wedding gift to us. She had met both my boys and recognized Alec's name right away.

"I guess it's big news," I said, and we decided to remain outside. We didn't want to talk to anyone, and we certainly weren't going to watch television.

That night, around 11pm, my mother pulled into the driveway. She had not met Lynn yet, and I wished their introduction could have been under more pleasant circumstances. She, Lynn, and I set up lawn chairs in front of the house. The night was warm. There was no sign of the media. My neighbors had kept their word, and I saw a Township police officer parked at the end of the street.

I still felt the calmness and strength from Friday morning in spite of the pain in my heart. I started to feel more and more confident that I would make it through and that it would turn into something positive. My mother couldn't believe how well I was doing and that I was even functioning. I tried to explain what had happened to me in the bedroom Friday morning, but it was too much for her to comprehend – she needed time to come to terms with everything else going on.

We talked about Alec, the signs some of us saw in him and what was going to happen next. Lynn and I invited her to stay with us, but she wanted to head back home. I don't think she wanted to be around for everything that was going to happen in the days and weeks ahead. Who could blame her? I didn't want to be around for it either.

It was after midnight when my mother finally left. It had been a long day.

Tomorrow I visit my son in prison for the first time, I thought to myself. *What a Father's Day this is going to be.*

It didn't feel like a day to celebrate being a father.

"Do you want to go to church?" Lynn asked me.

As much as I probably should have gone, I didn't want to go out. I didn't want to hear a preacher talk about fathers. I didn't want to have conversations or socialize or explain what had happened, what we were going through. I needed time before venturing out into a social setting. Lynn understood and went to church on her own. I stayed home.

When I woke up, Drew gave me a Father's Day card: formulated out of popsicle sticks and cut pipe cleaners, it was shaped like an open card and stood up on end. "Happy Father's Day" the card said on the outside, and "I made you something special" on the inside. I gave him a long hug and felt overwhelmed with thanks that he was there with me on Father's Day.

Around noon, I called my father and wished him a happy Father's Day. Our conversation was brief. He didn't know what to say about what was happening in my life or how to handle it. Who could blame him? What do you say or do at a time like this?

Amy came by the house in the afternoon, and I was happy to see her. I looked forward to spending some time with her, but as soon as she arrived, I noticed that she was agitated and upset.

"What's up?" I asked.

"Some reporter came up to me outside Mom's house. They wanted to ask me questions." It was all that she wanted to talk about.

"I warned you that might happen," I said. "That's why I invited you and your mother to stay here with us. Things are more private here, more secure."

She gave me a Father's Day card and a gift, but she kept talking about the incident, leaving the house after only a few minutes.

My Father's Day gift from her was a continuation of past gifts: a photo album. Years ago, my daughter started an album for me with some photos of her and the boys. During the divorce, all of the albums had gone with Diane, and I had been saying for years that I'd like to go through them and make copies. Well, my daughter started that process for me. It was a wonderful gift and meant a lot to me. She and Lynn had gone to Walmart while Diane and I were waiting to see Alec at the police station. There were many new pictures of happier times and great family memories.

I began looking through the album but only made it through the first few pages before my eyes flooded with tears and I literally could not see anything. Every picture of Alec reminded me of what was, what could have been, and what would never be. The photos of him when he was young, smiling and enjoying life were too much to see.

Where had things gone so wrong for my little boy?

Look at him. He's just a boy. He was happy once. This terrible thing that he has done — it's not the real him.

I closed the album and set it on the counter beside the card and picture from Alec as well as the card my youngest son had made for me.

Maybe someday, I'll be able to look at those pictures again. But not today.

24

"Should the Father
Receive the Reward?"

The warden made special arrangements for Alec's mother and me to visit him on Sunday afternoon, so Alec's mother met me at the house, and we drove over together. In ten minutes or so, we arrived at the Lancaster County Prison, a place I had never been. I didn't know what to expect. The warden scheduled our visit for 3:00pm, and we had 45 minutes.

We walked into a small waiting room that had only a desk, a metal detector, a few chairs, and a wall covered with small lockers. Later, I discovered the lockers were for all of our personal belongings – we couldn't take any jewelry or other items with us while visiting Alec. The room was empty, but in a few minutes, the warden arrived.

"Hi," he said, shaking my hand and introducing himself. "Due to the high profile nature of the case, you're being assigned a special visitation time. You'll have 45 minutes of private visitation, which starts at the end of normal visiting hours. We want to avoid disruption for your family and also for the inmates."

He paused.

"It's also a safety precaution for Alec. In the past, we've found that this type of case can create some, shall we say, volatility."

Alec's mother and I nodded. He handed us a pamphlet.

"This explains the dress code for your visitations, as well as other important policies and procedures." He went on to describe how we could get mail to Alec.

"Alec's being held in the Mental Health Unit," he continued. "He will most likely remain there for his entire stay: he won't be placed with the general population."

What a relief.

"What about his schooling?" I asked. "Is that finished because of this?"

"No, Alec will continue to receive his education, and we'll work with his school regarding coursework. All juveniles are required to continue their education and work towards their high school diploma."

This was good news, at least in light of everything else that was going on. Alec would get to finish high school. It was also a difficult reminder for me of all the things I had taken for granted that now would never happen: Alec's trip to Germany, his junior and senior years of high school, homecoming, the prom, high school graduation, visits to colleges, and all that his bright future once held.

"Here's my contact information," the warden said, handing me a card. "Call me any time you have questions about the facility."

It was time for our visit.

We showed our IDs, signed in, and placed all of our belongings in one of the lockers. The correctional officer then had us walk through the metal detector. All clear. An officer opened a door and led us into a very small room containing several doors.

Once inside, I heard the door close behind us, and the officer took out a metal detection wand. I opened my mouth and lifted my tongue. The man scanned me front and back and checked the bottom of my shoes. Diane was required to go through the same process. Then, he opened an interior door and led us into a much larger room that had four rows of chairs.

The two rows on the right side faced each other as did the two rows on the left. On the far right side of the room, an area was sectioned off so that visitation could take place with inmates on the other side of the glass. I looked around the room, and my heart sank. We were told to sit on the right side of the room.

Is this how all of our visits with Alec would take place? For the rest of his life, is this as private as it would get?

I heard another door open around the corner and out of sight at the far end of the room. A few corrections officers led Alec toward us – he wore a faded black and white jump-suit and looked exhausted.

"Am I allowed to hug him?" I asked.

"You're allowed a brief hug at the beginning and at the end, but no other contact is permitted during the visit," one of the officers said.

His mother hugged him first, and then I gave him a hug. He sat down across from us looking tired and unsettled. I could tell he struggled with his change of environment.

"What's it like in your cell?" I asked him.

"All I have is a Bible and a blanket," he said quietly in a matter-of-fact tone, as if talking about someone else's situation. "The light is always on - I guess because I'm on suicide watch. There are video cameras on the wall."

That image of my son sitting in front of me in a jump-suit, guards looking down on our conversation, emphasized once again how far he had fallen from the life I wanted for him. So much potential. Gone.

Where did it all go wrong?

How did we end up in this spot?

"We're here for you, Alec," I said.

In spite of not knowing what to talk about, the 45 minutes went by quickly.

I gave him a good-bye hug.

"I love you, son. Be strong."

Then, I sat back down and watched the guards escort him away. As he disappeared around the corner, heaviness overtook my heart. The day before had been difficult, but seeing him here, in prison: suddenly everything was very real to me. He now existed behind steel bars, concrete, locked doors, and he wouldn't be getting out any time soon. If ever.

I heard the loud closing of the door, and he was gone. Our visit was over.

One corrections officer remained behind and told us we could go. He escorted us through the door we had entered, and as we left, it closed behind us with a loud bang.

I know it's kind of a movie cliché, but when that door closed, chills raced through my body. That sound was a physical symbol, a reminder of where my son would be, locked away from the world, away from me. The door had closed on his life.

I arrived home to find Lynn and Drew out front doing yard work. She stayed busy that week to keep her mind off of things and tried to keep my son busy as well. He had spent the entire week with us, and Lynn was instrumental in keeping his life as normal as possible. She rearranged her work schedule, ran errands for me, and kept an eye on him while I handled things with Alec.

On top of all that, she stayed strong and supported me through it all. Her faith and love got me through many rough moments. She had spent the previous day, Father's Day, shopping with my daughter while Diane and I went to the police station. Lynn understood we needed to pull together as a family – not once did she complain about me going to Philhaven every night with my ex-wife. She knew how important it was for all of us to support Alec.

Lynn came over to the car when I pulled into the driveway. As we got out of the car, she asked Diane, "How are you doing?" Diane immediately became upset and began to cry, recapping the events of the past two weeks. Lynn reached out and gave her a long hug, and Diane just kept crying and crying. There was so much sadness and regret there in the driveway with us. I kept an eye out for my youngest son, hoping he was out of earshot. I continued to feel such a strong urge to protect him. I walked around the house and found him.

"Are you ready to go to your mother's house?"

He went inside to pack a few things and then came back out. By then, his mother had composed herself. I watched as they drove off, wishing he could stay.

I could no longer protect Alec, but I could protect his younger brother.

How am I going to get that balance right? I asked myself. He needed to be a kid, and I needed to trust him, but I felt this overwhelming fear that somehow I would lose him, too.

If that happened, it would be more than I could take.

I became so consumed with Alec's situation that for the first few weeks after his arrest, the outside world just went by without me noticing anything. I couldn't have told you any of the world news during that time or even what went on in our community. I focused all of my energy and emotion on my son, and nothing else held any significance.

However, I did notice one interesting change. My friends and coworkers stopped telling me about their lives and problems. I know it's probably because they thought their life couldn't compare to what I was going through, and they didn't want to bother me with their "stuff." But that didn't help me because hearing about other people's lives was one of the few things that got my mind off of Alec and all the problems surrounding his situation. I felt like all I was doing was taking from others and not giving anything in return.

"What's going on with you?" I'd ask people.

"Well," they would begin. But then they'd rethink what they were going to say. "Never mind. It's nothing compared to what you're going through."

No, please, tell me what's going on in your life! I'd think to myself. *I need to think about something else. I want to think about something else!*

This is how those early days after Alec's arrest passed.

On Sunday evening, a good friend of mine called, informing me that she was bringing dinner over and "wouldn't take no for an answer." She and her husband brought over a wonderful dinner, the first I'd eaten in a long time. They acted like they were just going to drop off the food and go back home.

"No way!" I said. "You've brought over enough food for eight people. We're getting this out right now and eating together."

They agreed to stay. Then, the doorbell rang: another friend and her husband had stopped by to see how we were doing, so the six of us hung out for the evening. It was a welcome distraction and some temporary comfort. We talked about pretty much anything except Alec and his situation.

Another day was over. Up until then, it had been an all out sprint towards an immediate goal. Now, I settled in for a marathon, waiting for the results of all that had transpired during the previous five days.

Had it only been five days?

Early on in the process I made a decision – I would not read or listen to the media when it came to Alec's case. I didn't need to subject myself to the emotional turmoil of reading everything that was going to be said publicly. I didn't want to constantly relive what had taken place, and I didn't need the angst that would overwhelm me at speculation or false reports.

My attorney did a great job as the spokesman for our family in those early days, making it very clear that we wanted to maintain our privacy. I was skeptical about the media and their intentions – over the years I had seen people subjected to public scrutiny and invasion of privacy while they tried to deal with some sort of family tragedy. My imagination ran wild with what might happen: reporters and media vans parked in front of my home? Constant calls on the phone? Showing up at my work or my daughter's work?

I worried about the public, too – would they criticize us? How would it all affect Lynn and the rest of my family? Fortunately, very few of my worries ever came true.

Not once did a member of the press approach me in public. Everyone went out of their way to respect my feelings and desire for privacy, including the media and local authorities. Even though my home phone number was publicly listed, I only received a few telephone calls. No one was pushy or intrusive.

My attorney kept me up to date on what was going on in the media. He monitored the news and the Internet on behalf of my family – there was no need to subject myself to the rumors or speculation that seemed to be running rampant. He shared things with me, so that I could be prepared in case questions came up. His intervention in these day-to-day details of my life helped so much. With no exaggeration, I can say I don't know what I would have done without him.

One rumor that surfaced during that time was that Kevin was gay, or that Kevin and Alec and been romantically involved and Alec feared that

Kevin was going to let their secret out. I guess it is human nature to ask why and to look for answers, but to spread baseless rumors is an insensitive thing to do. At the time, I wished people would stop speculating and leave the Haines family alone.

I understood and fully expected negative backlash toward Alec and my family. After all, look at what was taken from the Haines family. But there was no excuse to spread false and unsubstantiated stories that would be hurtful to the Haines family. I tuned it out, knowing that the people who believed this would have their imaginations captured by the next sensational story, and we would quickly become old news.

One night, the phone rang. I thought I recognized the number on caller ID, so I answered the call.

"Hello?"

To my dismay, it was a reporter. I could tell she was surprised that I had even answered, and she seemed almost unprepared to speak with me.

"Can I ask you a few questions, Mr. Kreider?" she asked gingerly.

"I'm not really interested in commenting at this point," I said politely.

I expected her to push for answers, clamor for information, but I was pleasantly mistaken.

"Okay," she said in a soft voice. "Thank you for your time."

I forgot about this conversation until one of my friends told me there was an article in the Sunday Newspaper that I should read. It supposedly had "good" things to say about me, so I decided to check it out. The front page headline read: "Turning In Your Own: Alec Kreider's parents faced the unbearable and did the unusual after he confessed to killings."

The headline was painful for me to read, focusing the spotlight on what had taken place. I found the full article on page four, with a different headline: "Terrible Burden to Bear." Just reading those headlines made me emotional, and I began to second-guess my decision. The article briefly recounted the events of the night of the murders. The latter part included comments from experts on how to deal with such an event. They spoke about how violence by our sons is becoming so common. But there were also kind and sympathetic words:

The confession took place Tuesday, June 12. Two days later, on June 14th, Timothy Kreider talked to the police. The agonies of those intervening days only can be imagined, as Timothy Kreider and Alec's mother have declined to speak to the media. Reached at his home Thursday, Timothy Kreider said quietly and politely, "I'm not really interested in commenting at this point." Lancaster County District Attorney, Donald Totaro, said in an email: "In 20 years as a prosecutor, I cannot recall another case where a parent provided this level of cooperation for a crime of this magnitude. Although some parents do report criminal activity as a means of seeking treatment for their child, we are confronted with many parents who obstruct police in investigations or rationalize their child's conduct in an effort to protect their children. Mr. and Mrs. Kreider were very cooperative with police, under extremely traumatic circumstances, and this community should be grateful for their courage."

When I read the comments by the reporter, I was incredibly touched and thankful. She had relayed exactly what I said and told the manner in which I said it. Something I had not expected from a member of the media.

On Monday, June 25th, I received another call from my family telling me to check out the editorial section in the *Lancaster New Era* newspaper. I had ventured out once, and the experience hadn't been too bad, so I decided to check this one out, too. The editorial's title was, "For Dad, Crucial Test of Character."

"Of all the properties which belong to honorable men, not one is so highly prized as that of character." We hope these words from Henry Clay, the nineteenth-century American statesman and orator, are a comfort to Timothy Kreider.

In what must have been an excruciatingly painful decision, Kreider called police on June 14 to report that his 16-year-old son, Alec, had confessed to the triple murder in Manheim Township that occurred four weeks earlier.

146

From there, the article again recounted the details of the case and the comments of the District Attorney. I was in tears after the first paragraph. I did not feel like a man of character. I did not feel like I passed any test or proved anything. All I had done was what I thought was the right thing to do, and that decision may lead to my son spending the rest of his life in prison. Nothing about what I did felt right. It had only brought pain, loss, doubt, and grief.

What about that shows character?

I had read the articles on Sunday and Monday, and the positive tone towards my family and me was encouraging. The local media seemed sympathetic towards us, a sharp contrast to my worst fears. The reporting was balanced, and restraint was being exercised. I felt relieved that none of my other children's names had been released, and for the most part, our privacy had been respected.

But reading that stuff was too difficult for me. I just couldn't do it – there was no need. It was the same information, and all it did was reopen the same wounds.

On Tuesday, the 26th of June, I felt like I needed to try to do some work, just to keep my mind busy. I planned on having lunch with a coworker to discuss the possibility of working from home. I was in the middle of bringing him up to speed regarding how I was doing when Diane called.

"Hello?" I answered.

"Hi. There's something in the paper you should know about today. The front page headline is, 'Should Dad Get Reward.'"

It caught me by surprise. My attorney and I had spoken about that very subject, and I made it clear to him that I wanted nothing to do with the reward money.

"Thanks for the heads up," I said.

I hung up and told my friend about the headline. He was dumbfounded.

Seconds later my phone rang again – my attorney.

"Just saw the article," Brian said, anger in his voice. "It's very inflammatory – my staff have me in lock down so I don't leave the office and do something I'll regret."

We both kind of laughed at that.

"How do you want to respond?" he asked.

"Let me grab a paper," I said. "I want to see what's being said. But I want nothing to do with the reward money. You know that."

"Yeah, I know. I'm on it. I'm going to issue a strong, emphatic response today and try to get a statement on the local evening news. I'll also contact the morning paper to see about publishing an accurate article. If I see anything on blogs, I'll respond."

I hung up, very happy that he was in my corner.

I stopped by a small local market on my way home just to pick up a newspaper. Besides reading those two previous articles, I had intentionally avoided the press coverage, but this was something I needed to see. As I walked into the store, I passed several ladies – they were employees of the store and stood in a huddle, looking at the paper.

"Do you think he should get it?" one of them asked the other.

I knew exactly what they were talking about, but I ignored it and kept walking.

"Well, I don't think he should get it!" the other lady said.

It was obvious that she was appalled at the thought of me getting the reward. I couldn't help but feel amused by the irony of the moment, so I slowed my walk and turned to one of them.

"He shouldn't get it," I said firmly.

Little did they know the authority behind my opinion.

I stopped in front of the newspaper stand, and there it was. The headline was in large, bold letters on the front page:

"Should Dad Get Reward?"

I picked up a paper and got in line to pay. I just wanted to get out of there and find a quiet place to read what was being said, but it was obvious by the reaction of these few people that this article was going to raise a lot of emotion and controversy in the community. As I stood there, one of the employees of the store approached me, and I recognized him immediately. We had attended high school and played baseball together.

"How are you, Tim?" he asked kindly. "Our sympathies are with you and your family."

We spoke quietly as I waited. We were just a few lines away from the ladies, and I didn't want them to know who I was. They continued talking loudly about the headline. My friend looked at me with an expression that said, "Man, I'm sorry about this!" I finally made it to the front of the line, and I leaned over and told him something.

"You can tell them the father doesn't want the reward."

With that, I paid and left. I walked out to my car, both amused and annoyed about what had just happened. Wasn't there enough pain in these circumstances without newspapers making up questions that had no bearing on the situation? I tossed the paper on the front seat and headed for home.

I walked inside and sat down to read the article: "Should Dad Get Reward: For some it is a sticky question." The entire article presented the story in a fashion that implied I wanted the reward and how the authorities should handle it. Statements and opinions discussed whether or not I deserved it. People from the community talked about whether or not I qualified for it. The more I read, the angrier I became.

It wasn't a sticky question! It wasn't even a question. I didn't want it. This wasn't journalism – this was fabricating a story where there wasn't one. A simple phone call to my lawyer would have confirmed where I stood on the matter. He had made it clear to members of the police that I had no interest in the reward. One call. That's all it would have taken.

But then I guess all of these newspapers wouldn't have been sold.

It was fairly obvious they were going to sell a lot of papers if the reaction of the ladies at the store was at all representative – even if it was pointless, inflammatory, irresponsible journalism.

I finished reading the article and called my attorney.

"I've already been in contact with the Lancaster morning paper," he said. "They are going to put our response in tomorrow morning's paper and will try to get it on the front page. The local television news station is going to run a story about our response, hopefully on the early news, but they couldn't promise anything. And I've been to the blogs and issued a response."

I thanked him and hung up. There was nothing else we could do.

Many months later, I would read my attorney's response on the local blog:

"At the outset, I apologize if I have not responded in the correct format, but I have made every effort to avoid contributing to Talkback. Until now! Many will recognize from my name that I am counsel for the Kreider family. As far as Mr. Kreider is concerned, he has never, ever, for the slightest moment, considered making a claim for accepting a reward. In fact, the thought thereof is absolutely offensive. The only thing more offensive is the New Era's suggestion that he be entitled to it. It is irresponsible journalism to write such a story, and to not at least make an effort to contact the family's representative and inquire of their intention...or lack thereof. If the Lancaster New Era cannot find anything else to write about, they should drag their butts out from behind their desks and do a little leg work. Several things were made public today which they completely missed. This wasn't a story...this was an obscene speculation by a lazy newspaper."

While reviewing his comments, I came across many people sounding off about the reward based on the article. Their comments and opinions were largely based on false information. Many of these reactions would have been very painful to read if I had looked at them at the time this all took place. However, I did stumble upon one voice of reason and sympathy among the heartless:

Thank you Mr. Beyer, for confirming what I've believed from the start. The man has handled an extremely bad situation as well as can be expected. He's done the right thing all along. It occurred to me that a man of this strength and conviction never thought once of reward money and would be seriously angered by the suggestion he "may" seek the reward.

Please, leave speculation out of any story on both these families.

And Mr. Kreider, You've been a rock through this. I'm very sorry for your predicament. I hope you get the privacy you need

150

in the near future. You`ve done the right thing from the start, stay strong.

I tuned into the 5:00 news out of curiosity in hopes our response would be aired. Sure enough, right off the bat they issued a report on the article and our response. They rushed to get it on, and the reporter wasn't completely prepared, but it was obvious they took extra effort to present our response on short notice.

By 6:00pm, they had it put together properly and nailed the piece. Our attorney successfully introduced our side of the story to the world, or at least our part of the world. The same segment aired again at 11:00pm. I felt better, relieved. All that remained was for the morning paper to publish a rebuttal – to me, this was the most important piece, since the original article had come from a Lancaster newspaper.

Wednesday morning, the first thing I did was to go get a morning paper. I spotted it right away, on the front page: "Father Shuns Reward: Attorney says Kreider family wants no part of $25,000 bounty." Included with the article was a picture of me from a press release that came out years earlier – it didn't look much like me anymore. I chuckled and was thankful for the out-of-date photo; I didn't want to be recognized when I went out.

> When Timothy Kreider told police June 14 that his 16-year-old son, Alec, had admitted slaying three members of a Manheim Township family last month, the furthest thing from his mind was the $25,000 reward being offered for information leading to the arrest of the killer.

> "There was never any intention on Mr. Kreider's part to collect the reward," said Mr. Kreider's attorney, who has also been acting as the spokesman for the Kreider family. "He never did consider it, and it is obscene to think he would want it."

The article then went on to recount the crime and give details about the source of the reward money. It finished with more comments discrediting the article of the prior day.

Their attorney said Kreider family members have been hurt by insinuations that they would accept, or even want, the reward money. "Anyone who has met the Kreiders as a result of this – police, attorneys, detectives – would think it's ridiculous to even entertain the thought that they would try to gain anything from this situation," Mr. Kreider's attorney said. "It is what it is. This family has no agenda, and to think that they do in any way makes it all the more difficult."

That was it. He had done an excellent job of setting the record straight: the truth was out now. There was nothing else we could do. If this didn't refute the prior day's article, nothing would. This was the last time I would read anything about the case for a long time. I didn't need to see or hear anymore.

25

And Then I Entered No-Man's Land

We settled into what became a strange, new normal. I tried to get back into the swing of things at work, and my boss and co-workers welcomed me back without fanfare. My boss adjusted my duties to help compensate for the time I had been away, as well as the mental stress she knew I fought. They did everything possible to help me through, help me put my mind at ease. What a blessing.

It had been several weeks since I'd been in church – I told myself it was too soon to go out in public, and I didn't want to talk about the situation, even with friends and family. Yet, I missed the comfort I felt in God's house. I decided I couldn't hide away forever – I needed to take some steps back to a normal life.

Lynn and I decided to go to her church that morning – it was just outside Reading and a little further away, but it was smaller than the local church we had been attending. It was a 7:45am service, which I hoped wouldn't be too full. We arrived a few minutes before the service began and sat towards the front, off to the left side. I settled in, felt good about being there, and wondered what the message would be.

As it turned out, the pastor was doing a series of teachings on a specific topic, and this was the third week of the series.

"As many of you know," he said, "this series is titled "Generations." We're focusing on how our family history can affect us and how we pass down our faith. Today's sermon is, "When It Seems That God Asks Too Much.""

"When it seems that God asks too much?" I laughed to myself. I was going to hear exactly what I needed to hear. Many times in the past few months, I had felt that God was asking too much of me, putting me through things I didn't think I could survive. I wanted to know what to do.

"This morning," the pastor continued, "we're going to take another look at the story of Abraham and Isaac."

It was like a punch in the stomach. I knew how much I would be able to relate to that story.

Abraham's wife Sarah was beyond childbearing years when God told Abraham they would have a child, and through this child, Abraham would have descendants as vast as the stars in the sky. Abraham and his wife were eventually blessed with a child. That child was Isaac, and Abraham would have done anything to protect this very special son.

One day, God spoke to Abraham and told him to take Isaac up into a place in the mountains and sacrifice him on an altar. Abraham was faced with an incredibly difficult decision. How could he sacrifice his son, whom he loved so much? Abraham prepared to obey God. He gathered the materials needed and left for the mountain where the sacrifice was to take place. As he and his son walked up the mountain, his son noticed they didn't have the normal sacrifice with them, and he asked where it was.

Abraham's response?

"The Lord will provide."

While the pastor walked us through this story, I thought about how I felt when my son's life was in my hands: the anguish of knowing what I must do, but not wanting to do it. Even with Abraham's great faith, the thought of killing his son must have tormented him.

Why this story? I wondered to myself.

Why today?

The pastor continued with his sermon, recounting the events in the lives of Abraham and Isaac, occasionally glancing in my direction. This is the

154

pastor Lynn and I had met with when Alec first confessed to me. He was familiar with our situation and had to know how hard this message was hitting me. Finally, he finished by telling us how Abraham remained faithful, and when he arrived at the altar, his faith was rewarded. His son was spared.

The effect this story had on me was immense and heart-wrenching. I had just gone through a similar battle. How do you sacrifice your son? The pastor talked about the emotional turmoil and challenges to a father's faith when asked to do such a thing.

I know! I know what Abraham felt!

All the pain and agony I had been through in the past month sat just under the surface. It fought to get out. The tears filled my eyes and ran down my cheeks.

"There are ways to deal with these inconceivable difficulties. What do we need to do when we think there is too much being asked of us?"

He went on to describe three things that might be able to get us through these difficult times: preparation, separation, and dedication.

When the time comes, we must be prepared to follow the path we know is correct. We may be tempted to stray or look for an easy way out if we're not prepared to do the right thing. If we're not prepared, it will be easy to look at what is happening and try to justify a course of action we know is wrong. It is essential to know ahead of time how important our convictions and morals are to us. Certain things cannot be compromised. If we condition ourselves to accept this responsibility and understand its importance, then we will be prepared. We must be willing and ready to obey God immediately.

Separation is another key. We must be willing to get away from what others are saying and doing. If those around us lead lives we know are improper, do not follow in their path. Do not judge or persecute, but do not follow. If a person isn't supporting you or is doing things to tear you down, you must be willing to move away from them. Do what you know to be right, not what others are doing or would do. If others are saying things against what you know to be true, do not listen. Do not let others influence and sway you from what you know to be right. You must "separate" from them.

Dedication was the third point. As Giovanni told Michelangelo, "Talent is cheap, but dedication is costly." It doesn't matter how talented we are or what our potential is. Are we willing to put in the work? Will we stand up for what we believe when things get tough? Are we dedicated to our cause, purpose, and way of life? We must be willing to stand by our convictions, morals, beliefs, and faith. It most likely will not be the "easy" thing to do.

Being willing to prepare ourselves, separate from the people and things working against us, and having the dedication to do what is necessary will carry you a long way. Will it be easy? Absolutely not. Will it be worth it? Absolutely.

His words challenged me, and I left the service determined to get through those difficult times.

At work, focus was hard to find. Alec's future was still up in the air, his only chance of a defense via the route of mental illness. This uncertainty became the toughest thing for me to deal with on a daily basis — not knowing whether or not he had a chance of life outside of prison weighed heavily on my mind. How could I move forward into a new future until I knew how his future would look?

So I didn't. Emotionally, I entered no-man's land.

Things around the house constantly reminded me of him and the things we had shared. Every time this happened, I wondered if he would ever get to do those things again and was reminded of the loss. If Lynn and I went out to eat, I'd think about Alec's favorite food or how much he'd enjoy that particular restaurant. Or I'd remember that I had wanted to take him there.

The grinding wheels of the legal system, slow and ponderous, offered very little hope of closure. At various times, the process appeared to reach a standstill. The county assigned a forensic psychiatrist to determine Alec's ability to put up a mental health defense. He had begun his evaluations. It felt like everything in our lives was on hold until we found out what was going to happen.

I was wringing my hands and rubbing my chest a lot, as if there was a physical way to soothe the emotional pain I was feeling. It was something I didn't think about or even notice I was doing until Lynn pointed it out. Even though she had made me aware of it, I was unable to stop this behavior. Lynn became more and more concerned about me.

"Tim," she said, "you're rubbing your chest again. You need to take some time off from work."

I refused to even consider this. Work kept me busy, and I believed I could power my way through this stage of the unknown.

There was one bright spot – I could still visit Alec. He called occasionally on the phone. He wrote letters.

He is still here, I constantly told myself. *His life isn't over. It's just going to be different. Focus on what we still have, not on what has been lost.*

For the first month that Alec remained in Lancaster County Prison, most of the communication (and especially the letters) carried a lot of emotion. Alec fought to deal with the possibility of being in prison for the rest of his life and the finality of his future. I tried to keep him positive, but at the same time, it became hard for me to hear him talking about maybe getting out.

He just didn't get it – he had this unassailable confidence that the mental health issues he experienced would carry enough weight to afford him a lesser sentence. He thought he would get another chance to experience life outside of prison. He began to appreciate the life he had, even though it was too late. I began to fear his reaction should he not be released. I didn't know what else to do, so I, too, clung to the hope that someday he would get out.

If he can be healed psychologically, he has so much potential. Maybe, just maybe it could happen?

Alec showed encouraging signs during those days: most importantly to me, he began exploring a relationship with God. When he was first taken to Lancaster County Prison, he had nothing in his cell except a blanket and a Bible, and he spent 23 out of 24 hours locked in that room. There was nothing for him to do but sleep, think, and read the Bible.

He was so desperate, and in this desperation, he turned to God for help. This initial exposure to God's word gave him strength and peace during a time of turmoil and uncertainty. We talked about these things a lot.

"Find your internal peace. Find your joy," I encouraged him. "God will provide you with a path to walk. If you do this, it doesn't matter where you are or what happens to you."

I knew that if he found faith, true faith, it would help him through what was on the horizon. He started reading the Bible on a regular basis, and his anger began to subside. But his journey of faith provided me with another personal hurdle to overcome – another stumbling block of guilt and self-blame.

In one of our early conversations, he shared this thought, "Dad, if I would have turned to God earlier in my life, it would have given me the strength and hope to deal with all those dark thoughts and stuff."

Immediately, a heavy curtain of guilt covered me.

Why didn't I take my kids to church more often when they were young? Why didn't I take my own spiritual development more seriously? I looked inside and blamed myself for all of it. *If I had done more, been a better example, none of this would have taken place! I should have been a better father.*

Alec must have picked up on the guilt I felt because he filled his next letter to me with encouragement. He listed all the things I did right for him and told me how much he appreciated and loved me as his father.

"I wouldn't want any other father," he wrote.

It helped, yet it broke my heart that he went through all of this before realizing how much he had to be thankful for.

As the process moved slowly forward, I started getting letters and cards in the mail. When the story about Alec broke, I had worried about this: would people go out of their way to find my address, or the address of my family members, and send hate mail? When the first few letters arrived, I opened them with some reluctance and trepidation.

It turns out my fears were not valid. I don't think I received any notes or letters with negative overtones– each one carried kind words of encouragement. I was deeply touched by the outpouring of support by strangers in my community.

I can't include every note I received – there are just too many. Here are a few:

Dear Mr. Kreider,

You don't know me, and chances are we'll never meet face-to-face. But, I am feeling led to sit down this morning and write a note to you. I have been praying for you and your family, and your son, Alec. And, I want you to know that there are many others doing the same.

We don't always understand why the people we love and care about make the choices they do, and I certainly do not completely understand why Alec did what he did. But, I do know that you love Alec and that your heart is broken. I also know that God loves you and Alec, too. Please remember that God has mighty big shoulders and He wants and expects us to lean on Him. I pray that you feel His love for you and Alec in a very powerful way during this very difficult time.

I hope you find comfort and strength in knowing that there are people in your area who are praying for you.

Dear Mr. Kreider,

You, your ex-wife and your son Alec have been in my prayers since the news broke. I applaud and admire your strength and courage. I cannot begin to imagine the pain you have endured or will continue to endure. Please know that as you face these difficult days, weeks and months ahead – people are praying for you and for Alec. He is not lost or forsaken. Many people are praying for him!

… I am a wife and mother of 4 children … years ago my… daughter found herself in some trouble. The support of family and friends, a great community, and my faith carried me through those difficult days.

I am a believer in the power of prayer. Please know that you can count on my daily prayers for Alec and your family.

Dear Mr. Kreider,

In the Sunday News article "The puzzle," it suggested that we "help each other." Beyond moral support, my limited qualifications to help with the tragic problem you find yourselves in, there is little practical help I can offer. I have found, however, that moral support can have positive results.

First I want to express the hope that sometime in the future Alec will be able to come out of the tragic present and have a better life at some future time. I hope that this new start will not be deferred too long

There were several things in the Sunday News that bothered me. One in particular was the "blame the parents" idea. The fact that Alec came to you for help indicates that this knee jerk answer certainly does not apply in your case. From what I read in the paper, you are doing your best.

You may be asking, 'Did I miss something?" In all probability you did. So did school friends, teachers, and many others. My wife and I were not aware of my daughters developing mental illness. It was not obvious...

I write this, not as a solution for Alec, but as a possibility you may already be aware of. Whatever your pursuit of a solution to your difficult situation, I wish you and Alec a successful conclusion.

Tim,

It is with sadness that we read about your son in the newspaper. Our hearts go out to the Haines family but also to you and your family. Nothing can prepare us for such shocking news but God is with you even when your heart is breaking. We have 3 sons and I can only imagine in a very small way how you must feel.

God is our refuge and strength, an ever present help in trouble. Psalm 46:1 NIV

He sees through the heartache, the confusion, the disappointment... He sees past the uncertainty, the pain, the brokenness... he sees beyond the here and now, to the healing, the hope and the peace...Jesus sees you – and he's closer than anyone could ever be.

Praying his love will sustain you and his grace will keep you.

The Lord is close to the brokenhearted and saves those who are crushed in spirit. Psalm 34:18

In my times of deepest anguish, I would read many of the cards and letters over and over again. Even though I often cried my way through them, they brought great comfort, the comfort that comes from knowing that people cared and didn't judge me or my son. Sometimes, I needed to be reminded of all the good and love that exists in the world.

26

Marrying Lynn

Those months leading up to the sentencing were difficult and draining. Alec's emotions traveled up and down, and I rode the roller coaster with him. He called me at the craziest hours, sometimes at 1am, sometimes at 4am. I'd hear the phone ring, and I wanted to take his calls; after all, he was struggling through a terrible time in his life. If he called, I wanted to be there for him. And he could only call when he was let out of his cell, which was usually when the general prison population was sleeping, so he didn't have much of a choice when it came to timing his calls.

But they wore on me, those early morning conversations. I was exhausted and having problems coping myself, and usually after we spoke, I couldn't fall back to sleep. He made those calls for a month or two, and I could feel myself going under. Eventually, when he seemed to be in a stable emotional spot, I talked to him about the calls and the affect they were having on me. I asked that he only call me during the day, and we moved on.

As time passed, the prison allowed him to have books and playing cards. He was permitted to read the newspaper, which wasn't always a good thing. This enabled him to read what was being said about him and the case. It would feed into various emotions that often made it more difficult to cope with his new reality. Once the fall rolled around, he started "school," and homework provided a small distraction. Because of the advanced classes he had been taking in high school, this coursework wasn't much more than busy work, but at least it kept him thinking, and boredom wasn't the huge problem it once had been.

His mother and I did our best to make our Sunday visits upbeat and positive. We looked forward to seeing him, and he was always happy to see us. But at times, our interaction seemed so odd – there we were, in prison, talking about funny memories or laughing about silly commercials. It was good to laugh together, yet it seemed inappropriate: Alec was in prison for a horrible crime, and his future remained undetermined. Was it right to be laughing? Did we have the right to act like nothing had happened? Did it trivialize the loss of the Haines family?

I wanted to enjoy the time with my son. I loved him as much as ever and only wanted him to find some moments of joy. But when the guards looked at us and saw us laughing, sometimes it felt wrong and out of place. Still, I put those thoughts aside and focused on Alec. He was my priority, and it was good to see him smiling. We would get him through this.

Lynn's and my upcoming wedding should have been a welcome distraction for us. Scheduled to take place only 45 days after Alec was taken into custody, the pending celebration had us thinking. Should we even go through with it in light of everything that had happened? Was it appropriate to have that kind of an event during such a dark time? But I was determined not to let Alec's adversity completely derail the rest of my life – what was going on with him was terrible, but I still had a life to live. Lynn and I decided the right thing to do was to stay on course with the wedding.

It was definitely a decision we made together. There was more than one moment where I asked myself, *Will she still want to marry me?* I wouldn't have blamed her if she had second thoughts.

We didn't want to spend a lot of money on the reception – we had a lot of other expenses to think about at that point. One night, while examining a few of the details, Lynn turned to me.

"We really need to discuss some of these things and make a final decision on the caterer."

I could tell she felt bad about how expensive the various options were.

"Why don't we just have everyone bring a covered dish?" I said, only half joking.

She looked at me, her eyes wide open, and I wasn't sure what she thought.

"That's a great idea!" she said.

From there, the idea blossomed, and once we got the RSVPs back, we contacted all the guests and told them not to bother bringing gifts – just bring something to eat. With a sigh of relief, we turned our attention to other aspects of the wedding.

Planning the wedding helped to take my mind off the pain and uncertainty of Alec's future. It was something joyous to look forward to, something to celebrate. But Alec's absence would be obvious and painful – he was supposed to be in the wedding party, and his absence would certainly leave a void in the day. I asked him to be part of the ceremony anyway.

"Why don't you write something for us to read at the wedding?" I asked him.

He said that he would.

When Lynn and I had first gone to check out Camp Mack (a local Boy Scout campground) as a possible location for the wedding and reception, we loved it immediately. The serenity of the woods and the peace in the lodge would provide the perfect backdrop. There was only one problem – a giant chipmunk stood above the fireplace. Not exactly a romantic wedding backdrop. Lynn said she would take care of it.

On Saturday, the night before the wedding, I walked into the pavilion to see how preparations were coming. Under the fireplace, I saw a table. And on top of the table was a ladder. At the top of the ladder was my beautiful bride-to-be, craning to cover the chipmunk with an elegant sheer.

"Lynn, get down from there!" I exclaimed. "The last thing we need right now is for you to end up in the hospital." She draped the fabric over the chipmunk and hung a grapevine wreath covered with flowers to disguise the rodent's presence. I couldn't help but laugh a little. Her will and determination were just a few of the things I loved about her.

On Sunday morning, the day of the wedding, I went to see Alec. I think Lynn was worried that it would get me down, but it was my regular visiting day, plus it was something he looked forward to. And to be honest, once I returned to Camp Mack from my visit with him and saw the beautiful setup, I was able to push all of that out of my mind, at least for a few hours.

Amy and Drew were already there and had helped with some of the last minute details. Amy pinned my boutonniere onto my jacket. She and Lynn had gone shopping earlier in the summer to find a dress for Amy to wear. She looked beautiful, smiling ear to ear. This would be the first wedding Amy was in, and we were so happy when she agreed to stand with us as we exchanged our vows. Soon, our family and friends arrived. Finally, the wedding began.

I'm not sure about the beginning of the ceremony, but somehow I found myself at the front of the pavilion, looking out across a sea of happy faces – the important people in our lives, many of whom had done so much for us during the previous months. They had prayed for us and fed us and stopped by to see how we were doing. They loved us. Thinking of how much they had supported us made me emotional even before Lynn appeared.

Then, I saw Lynn.

There was a long walkway that led from the kitchen to the pavilion, and when she emerged through that door, she seemed so far away. It took forever for her to get to me. Later, she told me that she felt the same way, wanting to hike up her dress and run to my side, but then she thought that if she fell there would be photos she'd have to destroy later. I'm not sure if our moment could have been ruined, no matter what happened. Seeing her, about to become my wife, was one of the happiest moments of my life.

After the ceremony, we walked down the center aisle to the song, "Some Kind of Wonderful." It was perfect. The whole day was perfect. It had been the celebration of love and new life that I had hoped for. When we reached the back of the pavilion, I closed my eyes and gave Lynn a huge hug – someone captured this moment on camera, and it is my favorite photo from the wedding.

We weren't planning on having a receiving line, but when I opened my eyes after that hug, everyone was lining up to congratulate us. It was amazing – they wouldn't be satisfied until they had each given us a hug and told us how happy they were for us. So Lynn and I stood at the back of the pavilion and hugged everyone.

As the band played, the reception began. The meal was amazing. Some of our close friends were excellent chefs, and they brought their specialties. Everyone else brought delicious food in huge quantities, and no one went hungry. In fact, there were enormous amounts of food left over. Everyone took their own dish home, which eliminated a lot of clean up. And almost everyone ignored our request and brought a gift along with food for the covered dish. We felt so blessed that night.

During the reception, my friend Chad did the toast, with his usual flair and sense of humor, and my daughter read a poem for us that she had written. It was beautiful and meant a great deal to Lynn and me. Then, I read the writing from Alec:

The Secrets of Life Aren't So Secret
By Alec Kreider

I have found that there are many things that all people should know, but we either overlook them or search too hard. In living my short life I have learned a lot while trying to be happy against the odds. The goal of every person should be to be happy. The question becomes. "How can we be happy?" All too often we think things that give us joy will make us happy. They cannot and they will never be able to. Our happiness comes to us when we achieve an inner peace. This inner peace comes when we accept ourselves for who we are; when we accept our friends and family for who they are and when we accept the world for what it is. Does this mean that we will never be sad or angry? No, of course not. Nobody can feel happy all of the time. Life's challenges will ensure that we feel tired and depressed from time to time, but true happiness is reliable happiness. When our stormy times have passed happiness will return if we have our inner peace.

What I have found is that there are several aspects to life that need to be put into balance. These are the following; work, Friends, Family, our hobbies/passions and for those who don't mind it, Faith. We must learn to love our work because we will all have to work someday in some way, shape or form. It has been said and I believe that there exists a way to make many different forms of work enjoyable even if we don't like the job. If, no matter how hard we try, we can't find it enjoyable then we should get different jobs.

Here is where we see the value and power of friends and family in our lives. The anger that I experienced in my more youthful days caused me to not appreciate my friends and family nearly as much as I should have. It took the most severe depression I've ever felt, so severe that I was only days away from taking my own life, to put me into a situation I couldn't control. The support of my family during this time (and even later into my time in prison) showed me how important family is. Not just to bring us joy, but to pick us up when we fall. Family supports us when the world has rejected us or injured us.

Because we won't always be with friends and family we need to have things to do in our alone time. This is where I speak of the importance of hobbies and personal passions. I have been a loner for almost the entire 16 years that I have lived. When you have a lot of time alone it must, I do mean must, be filled with things we enjoy or we go nuts with boredom or agony from doing things we don't enjoy. Plus our hobbies are a great venue for feeling more joy. From being in prison I have come to realize that the outside shouldn't have been so boring. I probably wouldn't have played video games as much as I did, but I can't take that back now. You might have to do some searching to find out what you like doing. I never would have thought I would enjoy gardening until I planted some flowers from a biology project. Oh yes, eat lots of chocolate, it's a natural happiness booster. That we all can enjoy.

This brings me to my final point: FAITH. What I have learned in my time in prison is that faith is a strong liberator. Can inner peace be achieved without faith? I believe so, but I'll tell you that it is very hard. In my time here, in prison, God has delivered another one of His ironies: Liberation in imprisonment. What I am slowly starting to understand is what inner peace really is. It won't come from our cars, our houses, our fine cuisine, diamond rings or anything material. You name it and it won't be what saves you from personal inner anguish. To be happy we have to love ourselves. To me it was no wonder that I was suicidal because I hated myself for the past 5-6 years. I won't lie, medication has helped me, but to truly love myself I needed support from God. The Lord loves me unconditionally. He doesn't care about the color of my hair, the perfectness of my teeth, how I smell or how well I can talk. He loves us for who we are. Something very important that I learned is God is always trying to love us but it is we who prevent Him from loving us by building barriers against him and being hypocrites. Regardless, we can find comfort in ourselves because we know that at least God will always love us. The next thing we can find comfort in is we have no reason to worry. We can do what we can then we have to let God do the rest and we know He will do what is right. That is the one thing we can count on. He will always do what *is right. We have to keep in mind though that He will do what He, the Lord, knows is right, and we must accept His judgment. Now that we have taken on ourselves we must deal with other people. I can again testify about this. Agonizing over what other people do is pointless because we can't control them. So all you and I can do is expect people to be people and deal with it the best way possible.*

There you go. That's everything I know about being happy. Get joy from the simple pleasures, love your family and friends dearly and do for them what you want them to do for you. Enjoy your work or come to terms with it; find reliable pastimes you love and enjoy and take a break when the going gets tough; learn to love thy self, whether by faith or personal wisdom, it does not matter. When things get tough pray and believe you will be heard and you shall be answered.

When I read this, it was hard for me to believe it came from the same boy who committed that gruesome crime. How could he understand so much about life yet most likely be destined to a life in prison?

Some people questioned if it was appropriate for us to get married so soon after what had happened with Alec. To that I've responded, "Life is about love and joy but also about sorrow. We do not have one without the other." If we permit the sorrow in our lives to control our actions, it will destroy the love and joy we were meant to have. Too often we focus on the sorrow in our lives, can't put it down or leave it in the past. We end up missing out on the love and joy waiting for us in this life, in the present!

Our wedding was a celebration of life, of love, of joy. Going through with it was the only possible response to the things going on around us.

Then, the wedding was over. In spite of marrying a wonderful woman and knowing I needed to be there for Alec, I was in serious decline. Things became increasingly difficult for me – the wedding had given me a wonderful distraction, something on which to focus my energy, but I was not able to move on or put away my sorrow regarding Alec.

I started getting worse and worse.

27

Rock Bottom

I functioned. I went to work. I ate, slept, and spoke with people when I had to. But I wasn't myself – I became less outgoing, more reserved. I wasn't taking care of myself. I stopped exercising, barely ate, and found it difficult to sleep. By the end of the summer, I was spent, used up. I felt fatigued and completely exhausted. Lynn's ever-watchful eyes noticed I was deteriorating instead of getting better, and her concern grew daily. She wanted me to talk to her about it, but there was nothing new for me to say. I had said it all many times. Finally, one day, I told her how I was feeling, what the magnitude of the strain and stress did to me.

"I feel like I am losing days off the end of my life," I said. "I feel them simply slipping away."

The constant unknowns combined with grief and loss beat me down. I didn't see any end in sight.

I had originally appeared to rebound quickly, but most of that was because I still had so many things to do, and the wedding had kept me distracted and looking forward. I thought that I could power my way through the sadness. I thought I could do it all myself. I stopped leaning on the source of the strength I had received on that Friday morning – that now seemed so long ago. I thought it was up to me. I could handle it.

Stay positive. Remain upbeat. Accept what you cannot control and have faith, I would tell myself, all the while feeling the love and support of family and friends. I thought these things would get me through if I could just tough it out. But I had underestimated the energy and endurance required. I just couldn't get back to my old self.

Perhaps I wasn't as tough as I thought?

Lynn's concern for me continued to escalate; her loving gaze conveyed the growing depth of her worry. It was obvious that in her heart she thought I was in much more trouble than I wanted to admit. This nagging feeling of self-doubt took root somewhere deep in my brain. What if I couldn't pull out of this? What if I kept moving on this downward spiral? What if I had an emotional breakdown or succumbed to depression? It became apparent to me that I couldn't process the events surrounding Alec on my own. This was bigger than me. I needed help before it was too late. It was time for me to follow the advice I had been giving Alec: seek some professional help.

The counseling helped to level things off and halt the downward slide, at least for the moment. I started to focus on the climb back up, out of the hole. But at the end of October, things changed regarding Alec, and once again I found myself clinging to the edge.

Months of forensic evaluations came to an end. The findings would determine Alec's future, define the level of hope that we might entertain regarding the rest of his life. The results, however, were not what we had hoped.

As many people had told me leading up to the findings, Pennsylvania has some of the most stringent standards established in the United States for a defendant using a mental health defense. Yet for months, I had put my hope in this – Alec seemed so disturbed, so mentally and emotionally ill, that I could only hope they would determine this was why he had done it. It represented Alec's only chance to have some kind of future outside of prison, even if it was 10, 20, 30, or even 40 years down the road.

Alec's treating child psychiatrist had been optimistic about a potential psychological defense, but his background was from New York, where Alec would have had an arguable defense based on his age and brief mental health history. But we weren't in New York. In Pennsylvania, it wouldn't be enough.

In one agonizing phone call, we received his final evaluation: Alec did not meet any of the standards set by the state of Pennsylvania for diminished capacity or insanity. He could not use a mental health defense.

Suddenly, Alec's future held nothing but life in prison without parole. He was 16 years old and would never be free again. I met with Alec's attorney and his doctor to pursue potential options, but we were all out of ideas. The forensic psychiatrist had determined that Alec was mentally ill, but not to the degree needed in Pennsylvania to use as a mental health defense. The doctor I hired to treat Alec agreed with the diagnosis.

"In spite of Alec being a danger to himself and obviously ill, he does not meet the standards established by the Commonwealth of Pennsylvania. There is nothing else we can do," he said.

Nothing else.

Alec would spend the rest of his life in prison.

This was a tremendous blow – I had been clinging to hope, albeit so small, but still, I had clung to it. It was all I had. And suddenly it was gone. At that point, I realized that I had to come to terms with the fact that my son would spend his life in prison and what that meant to each of us in the family. My greatest fear had become our reality.

My son's life was gone.

Alec's attorney had already told him the news, and he didn't take it well. After months of thinking he had a chance of life outside of prison, believing he would be sent to a mental hospital until he was cured, he now had to face life behind bars. His future was gone. He was so distraught that he began talking about suicide again and was put back in solitary confinement so that he could be closely monitored.

Our regular Sunday visits were canceled – they didn't think it was safe for Alec.

I spoke with him on the phone in the following days, and he slowly rebounded from the initial shock. He fell back into boredom – while on suicide watch he lost access to his books, letters, pictures, playing cards, and even his pillow. He didn't have a blanket, just the Bible, a smock, and nothing to do for 23 hours a day.

I became concerned about our next visit. I missed him. I wanted to see him. And I worried about his state of mind – being left alone with his thoughts, his guilt, his hopelessness. I couldn't imagine being in that cell for so long. The loss of privileges increased his depression and made things more difficult. What would I say to him when we were allowed to visit him? How would we begin our new relationship, one formed around the knowledge that he would be in prison for the rest of his life?

Two weeks after receiving the news, we visited Alec. Diane and I went in as we had done so many times during the previous months. We took our seats and waited. When Alec came out, four corrections officers escorted him. He wore the same type of black and white striped jump suit and ankle shackles. Diane and I hugged him, and he sat down. He was unshaven and looked exhausted.

"How are you doing?" I asked him.

"Okay, I guess," he said with an edge to his voice. "But I'm cold, hungry, lonely, and I can't sleep." It was painfully obvious he wasn't doing okay. It wasn't possible to change any of these things, so we did what we had done so many times before: we started talking about his brother and sister, the dogs, Lynn and the gym, basically all the things going on in the lives of the rest of the family. We talked about anything that would distract us from the present reality, that we would never see him again outside of prison.

How many times over the rest of my life will we relive this event? I thought to myself.

"When will they change your status?" I asked.

"I don't know. They won't tell me anything."

Diane started to cry. The emotion and reality of the moment became too much for her. Alec looked at her, and I could tell he didn't know how to react.

"Are you okay?" he asked quietly.

She took a deep breath and tried to compose herself.

"Yeah," she said.

Difficult as it was, she held herself together. I tried to keep things positive, to stay upbeat and encourage him. He could get through this. We all would.

"There's a lot you can do in prison," I said slowly. "You can continue your education beyond high school, read and write. You won't always be in your cell for 23 hours a day. Things will get better. You can live a productive life, one that matters, if you want."

Alec paused, looking down at the ground. He shook his head ever so slowly.

"What's up?" I asked him.

"Just thinking about the rest of my life," he said, looking up at me. "I can't believe I'm never getting out. I can't believe what's become of my life."

I have never felt so powerless in all my life. Nothing in my power would ever change this. I would always love my son – what else could I do? His path was determined. Now, we had to come to terms with it.

"I've been reading the Bible," Alec said, "and meeting with the chaplain. It's helping me, I think."

"Keep doing that," I said. "You'll find comfort from that inner peace."

We spoke for a little while longer then said our good-byes. What an emotional visit. Alec's mother and I walked out of the prison. But the weight of our time with Alec refused to lift.

The emotional strain compounded the following day, a Monday I'll never forget. The morning started with a call from Brian notifying me that an informant in the prison had come forward with very damaging statements about Alec. These statements would be used against him in sentencing and virtually insured three consecutive life sentences without parole, instead of concurrent sentences. This difference would make it virtually impossible for Alec to ever get out of prison, and if the statements got out, it would be traumatic for everyone involved.

This was the final nail in Alec's coffin. There was no doubt his life would be spent in prison. No future, no hope, no reason to ever think otherwise. Then around lunchtime, I received very bad personal financial news from my employer: a situation from a previous business deal, which I thought was resolved and had nearly forgotten about, came back to the forefront. Turns out, it was going to cost Lynn and me a substantial sum of money, $25,000! This added to the financial strain we were already under from the bills for two attorneys and a New York psychiatrist.

Later in the day, I went over to pick up Drew at his friend's house – spending time with him was the one bright spot in a world that felt increasingly dark. The news that Alec would never get out of prison, compounded with the financial hit, knocked out much of what remained of my emotional supports. Seeing my youngest would help me take my mind off of that stuff.

But when I got there, Diane was there, too. I asked what was going on, and she replied, "Didn't Drew tell you? He needs some time to think about things. He asked me to pick him up so he could have some space."

He didn't want to spend his scheduled week at my house. My heart was crushed. I asked if it was about the video games I didn't allow him to play: he and I had a disagreement on Sunday night about whether or not games involving killing people were acceptable. I felt they were too violent, and he didn't agree. When he came out, I could tell he was uncomfortable, and I tried to talk to him, but he just got into the car with his mother.

"Is this about those damn video games?"

I rarely used any bad language, let alone around my children, but I was on the verge of losing it after the months of strain and the other two pieces of news I had received that day. He wouldn't look at me, and they drove off. I called him almost immediately and apologized for what I had said and told him I loved him. It was another major strike against my emotional support system. It felt like I had just lost both of my sons in one day. This was almost more than I could stand.

Lynn called the house and could tell immediately something was very wrong. I told her about the day's events, and she asked if it was okay if she went to speak to Drew. It seemed like there was nothing to lose, so I agreed it might help if she tried to find out what was bothering him. She planned to stop at Diane's on her way home from work. When Lynn arrived home, she told me she chose to speak with Diane about Drew's choice to not come home with us, but that it hadn't done any good. Drew was staying with his mother. Within minutes of Lynn arriving at home, the telephone rang.

It was my daughter, Amy. At first I was glad to hear her voice, but it took only a moment to realize this wasn't a good call. She was very upset that Lynn had come to her mother's house and wanted to talk to Drew. Amy felt Lynn had no right to get involved. Little did Amy know that at that point I had no strength remaining to make the effort on my own.

Lynn simply wanted to try and keep our family together. My daughter lashed out at me for every mistake I had ever made as a parent. She was so angry and hostile. Amy told me in no uncertain terms that Lynn would never be a part of our family and that she would never accept Lynn as part of the family. Amy made it painfully clear she wanted nothing to do with either one of us.

My heart was broken. The financial loss barely mattered in the face of a family that seemed to be completely destroyed. In spite of all my efforts to save and protect my family, it appeared as if I had failed miserably. In less than 24 hours, I had "lost" all three of my children.

The combination of all these incidents in one day pushed me to the edge of a breakdown. That night a tightness filled my chest, and it persisted day after day. I would rub my chest and place my hand against it. My heart pounded hard and fast and wouldn't slow down, refusing to relent. The tension was unnerving. Once again, the comfort of sleep escaped me. Lynn and I went to speak with the psychologist I was seeing. He expressed concern about my falling energy levels and the other physical symptoms I was experiencing. So when I finally admitted, largely because of Lynn's insistence, that I might need some time off of work, he immediately agreed.

"Perhaps 30 days?" I suggested, at the prodding of my wife.

"No," he said, shaking his head, "I'm going to recommend 60 days."

"But if I'm feeling better after 30, I can go back right?"

"No," he replied firmly. "I insist. Sixty days."

I shrugged. The financial implications of taking time off or the ways it might affect my career - none of it mattered any more. I finally acknowledged that I needed to do something. I had to take care of myself. I didn't have the strength to fight the battle of my recovery and do everything else that filled my days and caused my sleepless nights.

Initially, it was a huge relief not to have to go to work. I could just sit and be – I turned off my mind as best as I could, tried to forget about the responsibilities I had left behind, and focused on what I had been through and the direction I was going. I slept a lot. For the first week or two, this intense exhaustion worked its way out.

When I had gone through my divorce, I spent a lot of time writing in a journal to help process my emotions. Basically, if I felt bummed out about something, I'd write about it that day and hope that somehow those words would create a path out of the pain.

But writing about Alec's situation felt different. It felt like a surreal story to me – almost unbelievable. I had to write it down. There was this compelling urge to write the story out. And it didn't emerge in journal form – it erupted from my gut in a narrative, pulling me along from beginning to end.

At first, going back into the story, to the day we all found out about the Haines family, I felt like I was drowning. Living back through those experiences and seeing them take form on the page initially gave me a sense of panic – everything was closing in around me. These horrendous incidents that had infiltrated my world would be the end of me, and there was nothing I could do about it. The pain and hurt were too overwhelming. I didn't have a chance.

But as I wrote back through those impossible months, I remembered one event that had given me such hope at the time. It took place the Sunday after our pastor preached about Abraham and Isaac. We went to a different church that day, one closer to home that we occasionally attended.

The pastor drew a line on an eraser board, and the line represented a life. It had mountains and valleys, jagged drops and incredible rises.

"Life is a journey," he said, "filled with peaks and valleys. There will be ups, and there will be downs. Some of you are at a very low point. Some of you are experiencing a high point."

He paused and let his words sink in.

"But it's the end that matters."

I knew at the time that it was another message I needed to hear. The pastor went on to discuss the four areas that affect our journey: circumstances, people, choices, and faith in God. The first two are aspects of life that we have no control over – I can't determine my life's circumstances, and I can't control how other people will think, act or behave.

But I can control my choices. I can choose to keep my faith.

The pastor went on to reflect on the story of Joseph in the Bible: how his brothers sold him into slavery; how he made a name for himself in Potiphar's house as a slave; how Potiphar's wife's lie landed Joseph in prison; how Joseph was faithful to perform every job set before him even when unjustly imprisoned; how he interpreted Pharaoh's dream and became the second most powerful man in the country; how he kept his faith. Joseph never let circumstances or people determine his level of trust in God.

At the end of the service, the final worship song began to play. It was "Storm" by Lifehouse, and the voice and lyrics set off a wave of emotions in me. The song is sung from the perspective of someone who is drowning, in over his head, deep in darkness. He doesn't sound like he has much hope, at least not at first. I knew how that felt. The words from the song perfectly described the place that I found myself in life: disoriented, unable to see a way forward, and doubting my ability to stay above the surface level of the raging waters.

But just when the person in the song nearly gives up, he has a realization: if he could see God, everything would be okay. If he could just see God There's a storm, but there's also a way to stay afloat. There's a light in the darkness, there is hope.

I wept. Tears streamed down my face as I struggled to maintain my composure. There was nothing I could do to stop the gut-wrenching sobs from rising up.

I've been drowning, I thought to myself. *I know what that's like. But will it ever be all right? How will things ever be alright? What's to stop this whole thing from dragging me down and suffocating me forever?*

As I thought back through that sermon, I reflected on the life-altering choice that was mine to make. It was up to me to choose happiness, honesty, joy, and love. It was up to me to turn away from hate, despair, and hopelessness.

If I kept my faith and trusted in the power and grace of God, I wouldn't drown.

I took off from work during the months of December and January. I wrote most of what you are reading now, and I got some much-needed rest. We were blessed with the discovery that I was eligible for short-term

177

disability, so paying our bills would be less of a struggle. I took deep breaths and tried to be still. I stopped trying to do it all on my own. And God met me in that space. My healing began.

28

Conviction and Sentencing

Meanwhile, the legal process took its time. We were stunned to receive a call that Alec's original attorney, David, died from a stroke, and we were saddened by his sudden passing – by all accounts, as well as my personal experience, he was an amazing man, and his death was a tragic loss to many. Alec trusted him, and it would be another hurdle to bring someone new into his shrinking world. It also meant that the court needed to appoint a new public defender and bring that person up to speed with everything that had gone on to that point. That took two or three months.

But as time passed, we became aware of the direction things would eventually go. Perhaps that's what made all of the delays so frustrating. Our lives were on hold until Alec's sentencing, but we all knew what the result of that was going to be. Still, we waited, because there was nothing else that we could do.

Finally, the date was set. Alec's sentencing would take place at the Lancaster County courthouse, almost exactly a year after the crime was committed. It felt so much longer than a year. Lynn and I drove over to Diane's house and picked her up. Amy also decided to come, in spite of her mother's and my insistence that it wasn't necessary for her to hear and see this side of her brother. It was the first time I had seen her since she cut me off over the phone. We chatted a little but mostly focused on the task of the day, making it through the morning and showing a unified family front. The four of us traveled quietly to Brian's office, conveniently located beside the courthouse.

We walked into his office. I felt weak and far removed, and the circumstances took on the feel of a movie about someone else's life. I felt that way often during the first year: seeing a newspaper headline at the grocery store that had my son's name in it; hearing two strangers discussing the case; walking into the prison to visit Alec. Even though I had settled into this new normal, I couldn't always escape the feeling that at some point I would wake up and it would be the day I found out that Kevin was murdered, only I'd discover that Kevin and his parents were still alive and Alec was getting ready for summer vacation.

"We're going to get you in and get you seated," our attorney said. "Don't talk to anyone. You don't have to say anything." Brian anticipated the worst: a media frenzy outside the court room.

We walked out a side door of his office into a narrow alley that ran along the courthouse. We entered the courthouse through another side entrance – inside, we walked through an unfinished basement level full of plumbing and ductwork and electrical panels. This was surreal and again felt like a scene out of a movie. He led us to the elevator, and we took that up to the level where Alec's sentencing would take place.

Stepping out of the elevator, I looked down the long hallway to where most people enter the courtroom. Everything seemed a little less hectic than I thought it would be. I didn't see any photographers, although I did notice a few reporters scratching out notes. I took a deep breath as we slowly proceeded towards the inescapable reality of the day. My anxiety increased as we approached the gathering of people, not knowing what to expect. Would they crowd around us, shout questions, demand answers? To my surprise and immense relief, it was uneventful, and we quietly entered the courtroom.

The courtroom felt small and overcrowded. There was a heaviness in the air from the emotion and presence of so many people. As Brian negotiated the seating situation for us, I scanned the room for Alec. There was no sign of him. Brian directed us to a row of seats just inside the door near the back of the room. There was only one row of seats and a narrow aisle for standing behind us, so I would have a view of the entire room as the events unfolded.

People packed in around the edges. I noticed a group seated in the jury box, and then I recognized a few of them: members of the Haines family.

180

Kevin's sister was understandably absent and would provide a video testimony. I sighed, again feeling the weight of responsibility for the way that Alec had shattered their lives.

We sat at the opposite side of the courtroom, just behind where the defense would normally be positioned. The press corps took up a few rows in front of us. The quiet rustle of muted conversation filled the room, and we waited. And waited. *What's the hold up?* No one knew. Forty minutes later, the judge came in.

Then, Alec entered, flanked by guards and wearing handcuffs and ankle shackles. His clothes made him look like a high school kid getting ready for the prom; he wore his only pair of dress slacks, my shoes, and my white dress shirt. He stood beside his new public defender and faced the judge the entire time. Expressionless. Staring forward. Not once did he turn and look at me or anyone else.

Days later, I asked him what he had been thinking.

"Dad, I was just trying not to fall over," he told me.

I thought it would be a simple affair. Alec had already pled guilty – the only thing left was for the judge to determine if his three life sentences would be served concurrently or consecutively. Diane and I had met with our attorney and Alec's new public defender, and they each told us that the district attorney was pushing for consecutive life sentences. More than likely, that would be the outcome, no matter what took place in court that day.

Kevin's sister had taped a video testimony that lasted maybe five or ten minutes. It was a very emotional plea and her anguish was obvious. Her family had been taken from her in the most horrible fashion, by someone they had trusted and welcomed into their home. How, if ever, would she be able to recover from this loss?

Then, two other adult members of the family spoke. Most of what they said no longer lingers in my mind. Understandably, they shared the pain, anger, and betrayal of what had happened. I cannot pretend to put myself in their place and feel what they felt.

The one thing that does linger with me is the assertion by one of the family members that they felt like they needed to "cut a deal" in exchange for the information I gave to the police. The anger and resentment in this statement stung me. Never, during all of these events, had I thought that what I was doing would be construed as improper manipulation for my son's benefit. It shocked and saddened me to hear that the way I had handled the circumstances seemed to have added to the pain their family endured.

Finally, the D.A. wrapped up the prosecution side of the case. He spent far more time on the "details" of the crime and describing the course of events on that tragic night than seemed necessary. Particularly since, from what our family was told, this hearing was basically a formality. Everyone already knew what the end result was going to be for Alec. Why would he put the Haines family through reliving those final moments? It was disturbing for me to hear these things. I cannot imagine what it did to the members of the Haines family present in the courtroom. It felt so insensitive. It appeared to be more spotlighting for the press than it was actually relevant to the fate of my son. Then again, perhaps this was only my perception because of the side of the situation on which I found myself?

After the D.A. finished his closing arguments, the judge shared his thoughts about why he thought Alec deserved consecutive sentences instead of concurrent. The whole process felt staged— we all knew what the outcome was going to be. Perhaps it helped give the Haines family some closure. I don't know.

The three life sentences would be consecutive. Alec would spend the rest of his life in prison. We had prepared ourselves for a long time that this would be the way things would go – there was even an odd feeling of relief that this part of the process was behind us.

The guards led Alec away, and immediately two women seated in front of me turned around to face us. I recognized one of them as a reporter for the local news station.

"Mr. Kreider, would you like to comment on today's hearing?"

But Brian stepped in between them and us and motioned for me to start walking.

"My client has no comment at this time," he said firmly.

I know we left. I know we walked out of the courtroom the way we came in and eventually made our way out of the courthouse, but I can't remember any of it. Leaving that place is just a huge blank in my memory. So many thoughts and emotions stormed through my mind: where would they take Alec now? How was he doing? How could the Haines's daughter ever recover from this? Where would our lives go from here?

Then, we were back in my attorney's office. That was a strange moment: Amy walked around the room in a daze; Diane stood off by herself beside the fireplace, sobbing; my attorney and I stood there talking about what had happened. Before I knew it, Lynn walked over to Diane and gave her a hug. She never ceased to amaze me. Throughout the entire event, her compassion, love, and understanding were unwavering. What would I have done without her?

"They don't know my son!" Diane kept saying. "They just don't know him!"

It occurred to me that they didn't need or want to know my son – why should they? They knew what he did, and that was more than enough. The Haines family and the public wanted to know he'd never have the chance to hurt anyone else ever again. That was all that mattered. Lock him away and forget about him. Justice will then have been served. I couldn't blame them for feeling this way even though they didn't "know" my son.

We lingered for a few more minutes, trying to process and come to terms with the events of the morning. Eventually, when the futility of continuing to relive the events became apparent, we left for home. As we drove away from the courthouse, we passed two dogs playing with each other on the sidewalk, both boxers, one full-grown and the other a puppy. The little one jumped up on the big one and tried to bite its ears – the big one held it down and batted at it. There was something about seeing those two dogs playing, oblivious to all the pain emerging from the courthouse, that made me pause. That image of those animals, so carefree, sticks in my mind.

What a year it had been.

29

Visiting Alec

It takes us about an hour and fifteen minutes to make the drive to the prison where my son is now being held. Alec used to be over three hours away, but after his transfer from the juvenile detention center to a medium-security prison, he is now closer to home. We park, and Lynn and I enter the prison waiting room.

First, we take a number, then wait for our number to be called. We give the officer our ID and fill in the visitor chart, listing our names, address, and vehicle information. Anything we have in our pockets goes into a locker – you can't take any bills in with you above a $5 denomination.

Then, we walk through the metal detector. Lynn tends to set it off more than I do. I usually give her a hard time about it and blame it on her accessorizing. The correctional officer at the desk stamps our hands with the day we are visiting, using ink visible only under a black light. On the other side of the metal detector, they swab our hands for drug residue. They swab our waistband and the area around our pockets, too, since that's the last place people touch before washing their hands. If we send in letters, they can't have any stickers or glitter on them, no crayon writings or pictures – sometimes people try to smuggle drugs into prison by hiding them in the adhesive of stickers, glue, or wax.

I wonder who thinks of this stuff?

You can't wear hoodies. Lynn can't wear anything sleeveless, too short, or revealing.

Then, we sit in a waiting room – it can take them anywhere from twenty minutes to an hour to locate Alec and move him to the visitation room. There are typically numerous other individuals waiting along with us for a chance to visit their loved ones. It saddens me to see so many young people and children waiting to visit their husbands, boyfriends, and fathers. Once Alec is ready, a voice calls out.

"Kreider can go on up."

We pass through a thick metal door and walk down a long hallway. Sometimes I think, *When I'm an old man, coming here to visit Alec, this is going to be a long walk.* I look up at the cameras in the hallway ceiling. I glance out the windows into the prison yard. I wonder who will visit Alec when his mother and I are gone.

They unlock the door at the end of the long hallway and check to make sure our hands are stamped. They check the paperwork listing the visitors and the inmate we are here to see.

Alec Kreider.

Then, we walk through one more sliding metal door into the large visitation room. I hand over the paperwork to the officer stationed there. Alec is usually already in the room, on the far side, waiting for us to arrive. He wears the same thing as all of the other prisoners, a faded burgundy jumpsuit with D.O.C. on the back. It stands for Department of Corrections. Alec walks over to the correctional officer and hands over his ID, and then, he is finally able to greet us. We are permitted to hug him at that point, with no physical contact after that until its time for us to leave.

The officer usually tells us where to sit. We all sit on chairs that are placed side-by-side so that no one's back is turned toward the officers' desk. I guess it makes it easier for the officers to observe and harder to sneak things back and forth. We talk about what he's reading, what's going on in the prison, what's in the news. We fill him in on what we're doing. They always interrupt us to do an inmate "count" – and sometimes if the room gets too full we have to leave early.

We usually stay for about four hours and try to leave before 1:45pm, when the correctional officers do their shift change. That takes 45 minutes and prevents any visitors from leaving.

After these visits, I've felt okay. Not great. Not depressed. Just okay. If Alec is struggling or feeling down, it can be tough, but he's been fairly upbeat lately, so it's easier on me. I worry about his safety, although he doesn't have a cellmate, and he seems to know how to avoid trouble. They generally don't have a lot of incidents at that particular facility except for the occasional "lock down" when he is prevented from calling.

Sometimes, I look at him and wonder what he'll be like when he's my age. When his hair starts to turn gray. I wonder how he'll change through the years, and my mind comes back around to that same old concern: I wonder who will visit with him when I'm gone.

30

Not Alone

I walked out in front of 250 kids at our church's youth center. They were all between 13 and 18 years old. When I looked out over the crowd, the sheer number of young faces invigorated me – when I see a gathering like that, I'm struck by the amount of hope and possibility in the room. At the same time, I am all too aware of the unspoken presence of pain, confusion, and despair so many of our youth carry with them. There is immeasurable potential for good in the young people of this generation, but they need to know they are not alone, and that what they are going through matters to the adults around them as well as to the rest of the world.

I scanned the room, wondered if there was another Alec out there.

Is there a child in the room who needs someone to intervene? Who needs to hear words that will finally push them to get the help that could change the direction their life is taking? Is there anything that I can say to keep the Alec in this room from moving forward on some kind of terrible path they might be on?

On that Sunday morning, I told them the story of how my son's best friend was murdered. I walked them through the situation in our neighborhood and then talked about Alec's state of mind. I explained to them how he threatened to commit suicide and ended up in Philhaven. Then, I told them about Alec's confession.

Very few of these kids knew my story. So when I revealed Alec's confession, there was a collective gasp in the room. I had to stop for a moment. I felt myself going back, my heart tightening, my eyes welling, but I regained my composure. I explained the compromising situation that Alec's confession put me in: stay quiet and let the investigation progress on its own or come forward with the information I had.

"There are two ways to live your life," I said. "The right way or the easy way. And they're almost never the same thing. Alec chose the easy way – he decided to try to face his problems alone, without talking to anyone. You might think that sounds like the right way, the tough way – tough people do things on their own, right? But that's just not true. The tough thing to do, the brave thing to do, the right thing to do - is to get help."

"If you admit to someone what you're going through, it's tough. You open yourself up to other people's judgments and criticism. You take accountability for dealing with your stuff. You risk failure, because now someone knows what you are going through and that you're trying to cope with it. The easy way is to keep all of it to yourself. And that's not the right way."

The room was silent. I could tell that my words were sinking in and making an impact.

"How do we know what the right way is? So often we are faced with a choice, and we decide what we want to do, what will feel good or simply what is the easiest. The good thing is that all of us have an inherent voice inside of us that tells us what the right thing is. The problem is that we often don't want to listen to it, because many times the right way is the opposite of what we want to do or seems too difficult. Our greed and desires override it, or the voices of the world drown it out and tell us it's okay not to listen. If we're honest with ourselves, we always know the right thing to do. The difficult thing is having the courage and conviction to do what is right."

Some of the kids nodded subtly as I spoke. Others stared, tears in their eyes. I kept going.

"There's something else to remember. Something very important: You are not alone. The simple fact that you're sitting in this room tells you you're not alone. You might be depressed or angry or feel bad about yourself, but someone else in here is going through that, too. Everyone in this room is going through, or has gone through, something: doubt, insecurity, fear, anger, loneliness, or depression. No matter what you are feeling, someone else in here is going through it or has gone through it. You can turn to anyone in this room and say, 'Me too. I hurt, I want to be loved, I want to be accepted.' You're not the only one. You're not alone."

"You're not alone, because someone on this earth has gone through what you are going through. They've dealt with it, they've been strong through it, and they made it to the other side."

"The second reason you're not alone is this: if you're in this room, there is someone in your life who cares about you, who loves you and will help you if you ask. You might think you're alone, but look around. There's a pastor, a teacher, a coach, a friend's parent. Maybe it's a therapist. Maybe it's someone on a helpline or a website. If you think you're alone, you're not looking hard enough. Don't get discouraged, don't give up, keep seeking. You are not alone."

"Finally, even if you don't believe the first two reasons I gave you as to why you're not alone, there's a third reason why none of you are alone. There is a power and love available to all of us. That is the love and grace of Jesus. He wants to be there for you. He wants you to talk to him. All you have to do is trust him."

Author's Note

It has been over six years since Alec's confession, and five years have gone by since Alec's sentencing. The years passed, and I waited to tell my story.

At first, I waited because it took me many years to get to the place where I could talk about what happened without being overwhelmed by a massive sense of responsibility. For the first few years after Alec committed his crime, I got caught on the downward spiral of blame and insecurity, wondering what I could have done to keep Alec from doing what he did. There was a constant voice in my head asking me, *Where did I fail?* Overcoming this powerful sense of failure was an important first step.

I also waited because I didn't want to sensationalize the story. There is another family whose lives were impacted in a far greater fashion than that of my family. They have endured a loss and pain that I cannot begin to understand, and they are a constant consideration in whatever I decide to do. If I was going to share my personal journey, it had to have a greater purpose than simply talking about the events surrounding this time in my life. It had to bring a message of hope and redemption to individuals, parents, or families going through difficult times. It needed to let people know that they can make it through the darkness and are much stronger than they may think. There is always hope!

But, in the end, I wrote it because I had to write it. This became more and more evident as I shared parts of my journey with others and saw the hope and redemption they took away from our time together. It was their encouragement that finally convinced me that it was time to share my story and that it was okay to do so.

There's a part of me that believes someone out there is struggling with something serious, and through my willingness to share my experiences, they might get help instead of doing something horrible. That's the main hope I have in writing this book, that it will positively change the course of at least one life. If this book saves just one community, family, or individual from a needless tragedy, writing it will have been worth it.

From the moment of Alec's confession to the present day, my path has been long and arduous. At some point, I finally realized that I wasn't able to cope with everything by myself and that I did not need to face it alone. A psychologist helped me process the events on an emotional and intellectual level. Visits to his office were a frequent occurrence for nearly two years and periodically thereafter. An unbiased, objective, professional third party, who made me feel safe to be honest, broken and confused, helped me to effectively deal with many of the challenges I faced, both great and small. He helped me work through the guilt I dealt with, the sense of failure and the deep anguish. Spiritual guidance from pastors and mentors also opened the pathway for me to find faith and comfort in a greater Power and purpose than what I could offer myself.

And I wrote! I wrote and I wrote and I wrote some more. I wrote when the words coming out made me weep and I wrote when the words didn't make much sense. It was one of the most therapeutic things I did, pouring out all of the pain and emotion on to paper. This book is a result of many of those writings.

At some point in the process, my eyes were opened to an incredible truth: we can't do this thing called life alone. It wasn't until I sought help from those around me and turned to God that I found a power much greater than myself, the power of faith and community. That's when I realized I could deal with the things that for so long I never thought I would move beyond. That's where I found hope.

During this process of seeking and receiving help, I started a non-profit called Also-Me and learned another great life lesson: when you are struggling and having a difficult time, one of the best things you can do is reach out to help your fellow human beings. Also-Me gave me a different level of purpose and meaning and even helped me to make sense of what

I had gone through. I became energized by the thought of helping others and turning my experience into something that would benefit those in need.

I did a lot of reading during the past six years and tried to spend time focused on things that were positive and lifted me up. We are fortunate, through local libraries and the Internet, to have access to a vast array of information on how to live a healthy and productive life, how to overcome hardships, and how to be a better person and grow as an individual. I immersed myself in materials on personal and spiritual growth and understanding. I prayed more than I ever had in my life and found a local church where I felt welcomed and accepted. Finding a spiritual outlet that encouraged and strengthened me was crucial for my spiritual and emotional health. This all-out effort to grow and heal personally, emotionally, spiritually, and psychologically eventually paid off in a big way.

This led me to explore the concept of forgiveness, which in time revolutionized my life. It took me years to forgive myself for the ways in which I felt I had contributed to everything that had happened. I had to forgive myself for not being the perfect father, the perfect husband, and the perfect person. The only way for me to get through these questions and doubts was by forgiving myself.

Then, there was my son, Alec. I had to forgive him for what he had done. I had to forgive him for the pain he had caused our family and the Haines family. Eventually, this forgiveness branched out into all areas of my life. It became obvious that I needed to forgive myself for a lot more than just the events I felt led up to what Alec had done. There was a long list of regrets: actions in my past marriage, ways I had treated my other children, things I had said and done that I never should have said or done. Then, there was a long list of people (parents, family, business associates, my ex-wife, and on and on) that for one reason or another I needed to forgive. It didn't matter the circumstances: if they were involved with my feeling pain, disappointment, or any other negative emotion, I finally realized I had to forgive them and let it go. In the end, I came to understand the act of forgiveness really was about me being angry or hurt because someone didn't meet my needs or expectations and not about them at all! This forgiveness truly helped to set me free.

People will ask me how I am doing, and my answer to them still feels slightly inappropriate: I'm in such a good place, emotionally, mentally, and physically. How can I be happy and thriving after everything that happened? How can I find joy in life after so many lives were devastated? Well, it didn't happen overnight – it was a slow progression, a long journey. For a long time, it felt like I had no right to be joyful ever again. Forgiving myself, forgiving my son, and going on a journey of spiritual and emotional healing was hard. But the effort was worth it.

Today, I'm happy. I can't explain it. There are still moments when I sit back and say, *I can't believe this is my life.* Occasionally the demons of the past return, and I feel down when I think of all the pain that was inflicted and how much was lost. Maybe that's why my happiness sometimes brings a lingering sense of guilt.

But I had to give myself the freedom and the permission to say, "What happened was terrible, but it's okay for me to move forward and enjoy my life." Because what is the alternative? Letting the past dictate my happiness today? All we have is today. The past is done, and nothing we do will change it. It doesn't matter how much we lament, play it over and over in our minds or continue to regret, it only hurts us. Wallowing in misery and depression doesn't help anyone. I know this is easily said and not easily done, but if I can do it, you can, too.

In fact, it's my responsibility not to drown, not to give up. It's my responsibility to myself and to those I love to become not only who I was before this happened but an even better person. And that has happened. In this process of healing, I've become stronger and more complete than I was before.

We shouldn't be so hard on ourselves when we experience difficult moments, even if those moments turn into months or years. But what do we do with those moments? Do we give up and let them win, or do we refuse to drown and fight back to the surface?

You're not alone. There are other people who can relate to your pain, people who are there to help you no matter where you may be. Refuse to drown! Maybe you are experiencing a significant illness. Maybe your marriage is falling apart, or your parents are getting a divorce. Maybe you struggle with an addiction, or you don't fit in anywhere. Perhaps your finances are a mess. Maybe life seems depressing and meaningless.

I don't have all the answers and haven't experienced exactly what you are experiencing. All that I can do is share what gave me the strength not to drown in the sorrow and anguish that came at the lowest point of my life.

Hopefully, this story will help you back to the surface. No matter how bad the storm may be, refuse to drown.

May God bless your journey and surround you with people who will love and support you.

Afterword

"Why?"

Even though this isn't what *Refuse to Drown* is about, or its purpose for being written, it is understandably one of the most often asked questions.

Why did my son commit such a crime?

I understand there are many reasons for this question being asked.

Some people are simply curious, while others are fascinated by the more sensational side to the story. Others want to know "why" because then, perhaps, we can prevent a similar tragedy from taking place in the future.

For others, having a why enables them to feel safe. After all, if we know why and the reason doesn't apply to us, then we are safe. Having a why helps some of us sleep a little better at night.

Unfortunately, as with so many tragedies, there isn't a "why."

There isn't a sensational reason to satisfy our curiosity. There isn't a specific reason that will enable us to spot the next troubled young person before they do something like this. There isn't a rational explanation that will make us feel comfortable in the knowledge that this could never happen to us, to our family, or to our community.

The reality is that a very hurt, angry, and depressed young man made a horrible decision. A decision that, no matter how difficult it might be to understand, was not based on any rational or logical thoughts.

So what are we left with?

Feeling frustrated because we're still looking for the sensational? Feeling hopeless because we don't know how to prevent this in the future? Feeling frightened because we don't know when or where this might happen again?

There is an alternative.

We can focus on loving each other. We can let everyone we meet know that they are valued and that someone cares about them. We can do everything possible to lift each other up.

I don't know about you, but this is the path I choose.

Blessings

Tim

Do you know someone who is struggling?

Are you interested in supporting organizations that help?

Would you like to have Tim speak at your church, school, business, or other organization?

Visit
RefuseToDrown.com

You're not alone.

Acknowledgments

Writing this book would never have happened it if wasn't for the patience and efforts of Shawn Smucker. He took the hundreds of pages of writings and helped put them into a voice and flow that conveys the emotions of my journey.

A huge thanks to Matt Roda from RODA Marketing for putting together an amazing website for us.

Thank you to Walt Mueller from CPYU.org for giving me Shawn's name and for his encouragement to tell my story.

I am grateful to Andi Cumbo for her editing and valuable input into the flow and feel of the story.

Thank you to Kaylyn Keane for helping us to secure permission to include lyrics for "The Storm."

Thank you to those who read the book and provided insightful feedback: Casey Sauers, Jan and Jeff Gernsheimer, Chad Neiss and Jan Lucca.

Then there are the individuals who have supported me and encouraged me through this journey: Lynn, my loving wife; Pastor Bryan Koch; Perry Hazeltine, PhD; Melanie Holland; Bob Beyer; Keith Walker; Dave and Jan Lucca; Ann Soudant; and Warren Sickman.

Thank you.

About the Authors

Tim Kreider is passionate about helping people find healing and wholeness. He shares his story at churches, businesses, youth groups and other gatherings, and he started a non-profit organization called Also-Me that encourages people not to live life alone. He lives in Womelsdorf, PA with his wife Lynn.

Shawn Smucker is the author of eight books, including *Dying Out Loud, How to Use a Runaway Truck Ramp,* and *Building a Life Out of Words*. Stories are his life. Shawn lives in Lancaster, PA, with his wife and children.

CPSIA information can be obtained at www.ICGtesting.com
Printed in the USA
LVOW10s1655200414

382465LV00014B/1068/P